Beyond Small Talk

Five conversations that will change how you lead

Naomi Regan and
Lynsey Kitching

Beyond Small Talk

Hardback ISBN 978-1-917490-26-9

Paperback ISBN 978-1-917490-20-7

eISBN 978-1-917490-21-4

Published in 2026 by Right Book Press

Printed in the UK in April 2026

Manufactured by
Sue Richardson Associates Ltd.
Studio 6,
9, Marsh Street
Bristol
BS1 4AA

info@therightbookcompany.com

A CIP record of this book is available from the British Library.

This book does something rare in the leadership genre: it treats conversations not as soft skills, but as the primary developmental medium through which leaders grow themselves and those around them. It cuts through jargon and myth-making to show how our mindset, adult-learning dynamics and blind spots shape every interaction we have at work.

Dr Alis Anagnostakis, founder, Vertical Development Institute

It's refreshing to see such a core part of our ability to connect with other people given comprehensive attention. Too often we overlook the simple moments that lie at the heart of our ability to lead others and perform at work.

Andy Lopata, author of books including *The Financial Times Guide to Mentoring* and host of the Connected Leadership Podcast

This well-researched, practical and thoughtful book draws on human stories to explore five key workplace conversations that all leaders will recognise as being crucial to improving leadership impact.

Prof. Sue Dopson, professor of organisational behaviour, Saïd Business School, University of Oxford

This reframes everyday conversations as a powerful – and often underestimated – differentiator in leadership. At a time when digital communication risks eroding authentic human connection, their real-world insights remind us that meaningful dialogue is a leader's most scalable advantage. A must-read!

Camille Nicita, entrepreneurial business leader, mentor and board member

I love the concept, I love the challenge it poses and I love the fact that it is a practical handbook where you feel as though you are in a conversation with the authors. Communicating well at work does not come naturally to all, but this book will walk with you on that journey.

Dr Gail Carson OBE, researcher and practitioner, University of Oxford

For founder-led teams racing to scale, it's pure gold: practical, quick to use and brilliant at helping founders stop being the bottleneck. This should be a permanent fixture on your business bookshelf — warm, no-nonsense and reassuringly comforting.

James Cole, Panache Cruises, founder and CEO

Conversations matter! Naomi and Lynsey have gathered a bucket load of simple and easy-to-use ideas that will change the way you have conversations at work.

Claire Pedrick, author of *Simplifying Coaching* and *The Human Behind the Coach*

Leaders don't need to have all the answers but they do need to know how to foster the conversations that can help solutions emerge. This book makes knowing how to do so a learnable skill set. Simple, practical and immediately applicable, it's going to be really useful for anyone in a leadership position.

Ian McDermott, international consultant, bestselling author, founder of International Teaching Seminars

Beyond Small Talk reflects a coaching-led approach to leadership, offering practical questions and reflections leaders can use every day. This book makes a thoughtful, credible contribution to leadership practice.

The Coaching Academy

Contents

For Grace, Albie, Freya and Georgia, always.

Introduction

Why we wrote this book

Naomi writes: I vividly remember grabbing a book from the 'top ten business books of the week' shelf at the station as I was waiting for my train. The book that drew me in? *Harvard Business Review*'s *Management Tips* (2011). I still have it on my bookshelf, a good reminder of that moment. I recall sitting for the two-hour train journey attempting to cram and digest as much as I could before I arrived at the office.

It was week two of my first role as a manager and I felt sick about how completely out of my depth I thought I was. Two weeks earlier, I'd arrived at work confident and clear on what mattered, making tough decisions with the information I had and pulling in support when I needed it. As an engineer, I knew what was expected of me and the value I added. As a manager and leader, I didn't have a clue. So I reached for what I thought I needed: knowledge, tactics, theory. And I set about doing what had served me at every new stage of my career so far: studying, learning, gaining knowledge.

Did the book help? Would we have written the book you're reading now if it had?

No. Because what we came to realise is that knowledge and theory are nowhere near enough.

Fast-forward to today, and this is the book we wished we could have read, or actually the conversation we wished someone had had with us. It bottles everything we believe in and stand for: that conversations are the everyday building blocks of leadership, yet too many leaders avoid them, rush them or miss the chance to use them well.

> Leadership isn't about big, rare moments – it's about the small, repeated conversations that shape trust, performance and culture.

And whether you like the 'c' word or not, there's no getting away from the fact that culture is the glue that holds organisations together and makes good things happen.

Why conversations matter more than anything else you do as a leader

Let's start with a potentially career-limiting truth.

We run leadership development programmes for a living, so we recognise that what we're about to write next is potentially career limiting, but here goes...

What if we scrapped every single leadership training programme tomorrow? What if we removed every leadership theory book from the shelves? No more models and frameworks. No more research. What would happen? Chaos? Bad leadership? Or... would anyone even notice?

Our view is this:

> Most leaders know too much, but do too little of the things that really matter.

At CAPE People Development, the company we co-founded almost 15 years to the day after we first met, we have worked with hundreds of leaders across sectors and countries worldwide, and here's what we've learned: it isn't MBAs or formal qualifications that change things. It's conversations – real ones, human-to-human ones – that matter. But too often, those conversations don't happen.

And it's not just important at an individual level. Across teams and organisations, no matter the country, sector or size, one thing always stands out: *nothing has a bigger impact on what you can achieve than the conversations you have (or don't have):*

- the conversations that shape your career
- the conversations that support your growth and the growth of those you lead
- the conversations that feel hard, but you *know* you need to have
- the conversations you assume you've had... but haven't
- the conversations that happen once in a while and the ones that happen every day.

So, if conversations are core to leadership, you'd think we'd all be great at them by now...

If having great conversations at work was easy, this book wouldn't exist

Most leaders don't struggle because they lack intelligence, technical skills or experience. They struggle because:

- **they assume conversations are just *common sense*.** If good communication were instinctive, why do so many people struggle to give feedback, avoid difficult conversations or leave meetings feeling unheard? The reality is that just because you talk every day doesn't mean you always do it well.
- **they avoid difficult conversations.** Whether it's setting expectations or boundaries, addressing performance issues or

checking in on how someone's really doing, do you often put off the conversations that matter most, hoping the problem will go away? It rarely does.

- **they focus too much on *what* to say, not *how* to be.** Do you get stuck trying to find the perfect words or framework? Great conversations are about being present, having a positive intent and creating space for real dialogue.
- **they don't see conversations as *real work*.** They can feel like distractions from *getting things done*. There's always something urgent to do, a deadline to meet. So maybe you tell yourself you'll *find time* for a conversation later? But conversations are the work of leadership.
- **they underestimate the power of small moments.** It's not just the big, formal conversations that shape performance; it's the everyday interactions, the check-ins, the quick clarifications. These moments build trust, engagement and momentum more than you might realise.
- **they think saying it once is enough.** A single conversation rarely creates lasting change. People don't just hear something and instantly adjust. Growth, clarity and alignment happen through ongoing dialogue, not one-off discussions.
- **they assume they've been clear, when they haven't.** What you might say isn't

always what others hear, leading to confusion, frustration and unmet expectations.

- **they hesitate.** Do you know the conversation needs to happen, but second-guess yourself? This could lead to inaction or conversations that don't quite land as they were intended.

These challenges are universal, but they're also fixable. And that's exactly what this book is here to help you with. Our work with leaders globally has shown us that the same five conversations make the biggest difference. This book shares them and how to hold each one with confidence.

> Our workplaces need more confident, effective and impactful leaders, but to do that we all have to become better at having great conversations.

If you only remember one thing: conversations are the work of leadership! Leadership is lived in the conversations you have every day and the ones you avoid.

This book won't give you a script. But it will help you build confidence and skill in the most important tool you have as a leader: the conversations you have. Every. Single. Day.

Who are we to say this?

You could say we grew up in business together. Our career paths are similar; our experiences different but parallel. But our passion for learning, growing and supporting the growth of others is completely aligned. Naomi initially trained as an engineer, while Lynsey trained as a chartered surveyor. We entered the world of work in our early twenties, bright eyed and bushy tailed, eager to deliver great results. We'd studied hard, developed technical skills in the classroom and put them into practice out on site.

Then, around a similar time to each other, as we were good at what we did, we were both asked to manage teams. And in doing so we had to answer the common question:

> How do I move from being good at what I do to helping others to be good at what they do?

This career transition was a pivotal moment for both of us (although we probably didn't fully realise it at the time), and we know it is for many of the leaders we now work with too. The skills and strengths that had brought us success so far weren't going to get us through what came next, but no one told us that or what to do instead.

And at the heart of this transition (and leadership as a whole) was something we had underestimated: the importance and power of conversations. To be able to lead, influence and get things done through others, we needed more than technical expertise.

We needed better conversations.

Through CAPE, we've seen the challenges we faced ourselves play out again and again. We've worked with thousands of individuals, teams and organisations – from graduates to founders and CEOs, and everyone in between, helping them to make work more human and leadership have more impact. The result? Leaders having more and better conversations, teams performing at higher levels and organisations building the kinds of cultures that allow them to thrive.

Leaders we've worked with often describe the shift like this:

- 'The biggest shift for me was realising I don't need to have all the answers. My job is to have the conversations that get us to them.'
- 'I thought leadership was about strategy and decisions. But I've learned it's actually about the conversations I have – they're the only way anything actually happens.'

We bring our shared experience to this book: what we wished someone had told us earlier in our leadership roles and what we've been honing ever since. In essence, it distils the conversations that make the biggest difference to leaders, teams and organisations everywhere.

Who this book is for and the impact we want it to have

You might have picked up this book because:

- you're like me (Naomi) at the train station in week two, a manager doubting yourself (if this is you we want to say: you've got this and we hope the book helps)
- you know that leadership is about people but you feel unprepared for the human side or you don't know what that looks like day to day
- you're avoiding conversations you need to have or only having them when it's too late
- you feel stretched, are firefighting or stuck being the fixer of everyone's problems, unsure of how to get others to take more ownership
- you want to get the best out of others and help people feel motivated, but don't know what that means in practice
- you work with great people that you want to keep, but there are no promotion opportunities so you're worried they'll leave
- you've tried other books and found them overwhelming or removed from reality.

Whatever your reason, we want to make leadership feel more human, more practical and more doable. This book is here to give you more clarity, confidence and simple ways to have the conversations you might have been avoiding or overcomplicating, and to lead in a way that allows others to feel confident, clear and valued.

Whatever your role, if you depend on others to get stuff done, then this book is for you.

When we were asked what success for this book looks like to us, the answer had nothing to do with the number of copies we'd sell (though lots would be nice). Success is leaders telling us they used it and it gave them the confidence to have a conversation they'd been putting off. That it helped them see their role differently. That it didn't just change what they did but also how they thought of themselves as a leader, and they maybe felt a bit lighter in the process.

And when leaders do that, the ripple effect is measureable: clearer expectations, stronger and more connected teams, faster decisions at the right level, and organisations that perform better and can scale because people are actually talking to each other.

And if it does achieve those things, please tell us, as that's what gets us out of bed in the morning.

> The moment your work relies on other people, whether you manage two direct reports, lead a department, run an organisation or simply need colleagues to contribute to a project, the same principle applies: conversations are the work that makes this happen.

Why we don't care for the leader vs manager debate

Whether you call yourself a leader or a manager, we don't care. What we care about is whether you need other people to get stuff done. If you do, then you need to be having conversations.

The leader vs manager debate is a distraction that keeps coming back. Whole articles, courses and social media posts argue about the difference. But in practice? Does it matter? Not for what we're discussing in this book.

We hope you'll find this book refreshingly simple in many ways, and the same goes for our take on this debate. It's not about hierarchy, titles or semantics. It's for anyone whose success depends on others and who wants to get better at the conversations that make that possible.

In this book, we have chosen to mostly use the word *leader*. That doesn't mean *manager* isn't important. Of course, managing tasks, priorities and people is part of the job. But *leader* captures the broader, human work that runs through every role where your success depends on others. So when you see *leader*, read it as shorthand for anyone who needs other people to get things done, whatever their title and level.

How this book is structured

This book has two parts.

- **Part 1: Why conversations matter more than anything** lays the foundations. It sets out our approach, gets under the skin of what really happens in great conversations and tackles the barriers that so often get in the way. By doing this we introduce a simple way to approach the hardest part of leadership: our everyday conversations. The aim of these chapters is to help you make the mindset and behaviour shifts that allow the practical tools in Part 2 to work.
- **Part 2: The five key workplace conversations in action** takes a detailed look at the conversations themselves. Each chapter focuses on one of the five key workplace conversations that make the biggest difference: connection, clarity and alignment, development, performance improvement and problem solving (aka not fixing everyone's problems for them). In each chapter we break the conversation down to its component parts and then put it all back together with practical ways to use it straight away. You'll find a consistent structure so you can quickly get what you need: *when the conversation matters most, how to get started* and *practical tips, tools and reflections to make it work in real life.*

Part 1 gives you the mindset and behaviour shift; Part 2 gives you the practical tools to put it into action. Together they make the whole.

How to use this book

This book won't give you a checklist to tick off. There isn't a simple formula or a shortcut to great leadership. If it were that easy, you wouldn't need this book or the thousands of others out there on leadership.

You also won't find scripts or theory for theory's sake. This book is conversational, grounded in real work and focused on what actually helps. Our aim is to make conversations easier to have, not more complicated.

This book isn't a manual to follow step by step or read cover to cover. There's no *perfect* way to use it. Think of it more like a toolkit, ready with what you need, whenever it's useful. Here's how we think you might get the most from it.

- **Start with Part 1:** These four chapters are your foundations. The first time you read them they're probably best read in order (with a highlighter and sticky notes to hand).
- **Don't read Part 2 in order:** This part takes the form of a workbook. Use it as you need it. That might be the chapter that matters most to you right now or the one that feels the most familiar as a comfortable place to start.

- **Make it practical:** Part 2 includes exercises, reflections and things to try. So don't just read them, use them. Commit to at least one thing you'll put into practice each time.
- **Keep notes:** While there is space to capture your notes and thoughts in Part 2 (and we're huge advocates of marking up books as you go), you might prefer to have a notebook to hand to capture your actions and reflections, and also what you learn as you try things out.
- **Little and often:** Like conversations, the more you use this book in small, everyday moments, the more usable it will feel and the more impact you'll see.

This is your book to use in the way that works best for you. The most important thing is to put it to work, with your teams, with your colleagues, in real life. So don't just read it, use it. Pick a conversation, try it and see what shifts. That's how you'll see the impact: in how you and the people you work with grow, one conversation at a time.

Growth, one conversation at a time

We'll be talking about growth throughout this book, because your growth and impact as a leader (and as a person more broadly) happens through experience. Through discomfort. Through getting it wrong, trying again and learning as you go. Growth comes from discovering more about yourself and those around you.

Your ability to navigate challenges, lead others and create impact isn't just about what you *know*. It's about how you *connect*. How you listen, how you guide, how you influence. And all of that happens *through conversations*.

Growth, in this book, doesn't just mean climbing the career ladder or learning new things. It means shifting how you think, what you believe and how you behave. That's what these conversations help you do.

Growth for us is about:

- developing the agility to take on new challenges, in new ways
- taking responsibility not just for what you do but also how you lead and support others
- building the resilience to navigate complexity and stay connected in the messiness
- seeing that relationships are at the core of our work and strengthening them, one conversation at a time.

This book is about these conversations. Whether you're leading a team, stepping up into a new role or simply want to have more impact in the way you work with others, this book is for you.

A few words to keep in mind

A few words will come up again and again in this book. Think of them as threads woven throughout, so let's get familiar with them now.

- **Intentionality:** the best conversations don't happen by accident.
- **Reflection:** to learn and grow, you need to look back as well as forward.
- **Curiosity:** you don't have to be the expert; asking can be more useful than answering.
- **(It) depends:** people are complex and context matters.
- **Mindset:** how you see a situation shapes what you do and how you show up.

And here's one more:

- **Consistency:** one big one-off conversation doesn't change things – small, regular interactions do.

These ideas and principles run through the whole book and through the five conversations that are each simple in theory, easy to overlook and game-changingly powerful when done well.

This book will give you everything you need to understand them and put them into practice.

> Conversations don't just happen. But they do shape everything: how people work together, the performance level achieved and how people feel about their work.

So let's get started...

Part 1

Why conversations matter more than anything

Chapter 1

Why conversations are the work of leadership

Lynsey writes: When I first stepped into leading a team outside my specialism, the gap felt huge. I had trained as a property surveyor, but now I was responsible for a group focused on internal communications and change.

My instinctive response? To dive into the detail. I scrutinised everything my team did, read every piece of theory I could find, joined every meeting, even took on some of the delivery myself. Six months in (over a glass of wine after an event), one of my team members told me bluntly: 'I thought you were an awful manager when you first started. I wondered how I was going to work with you. I felt like I wasn't trusted.'

The feedback stung, mostly because it was true. I had been managing as though I was there to deliver rather than to lead. What was missing wasn't competence or hard work; it was conversations. With hindsight, what the team needed wasn't someone proving their expertise – they needed a leader who asked more questions, listened more, helped them develop and gave them the confidence to do their best work.

And that's the shift this chapter is about. Leadership isn't about doing it all yourself. It's about having the conversations and creating the space for others to have them to make it possible for people to deliver.

And while my story is one example, it's far from unique. In fact, it's something we both talk to leaders about on a weekly, if not daily, basis. This shift, from being the expert, the starter–finisher, the one with all the detail, is often the biggest career leap people face. But it's not the only one. You might be:

- moving from education to work, where the conversation shifts from receiving instruction to collaboration
- becoming an expert in your role, where conversations help you build credibility and influence
- setting up a business, where every conversation with customers, partners or investors can shape your success or survival
- moving from being an individual contributor to delivering through others, where conversations become about setting expectations and creating clarity for others

- managing a team, where the quality of your conversations creates trust, motivation and performance day to day
- leading a department, where conversations are about alignment, connecting priorities across teams and breaking down silos
- leading organisations, where conversations set the tone and culture, shaping how people feel and how the business is experienced inside and out.

Career success doesn't mean ticking off every transition on this list. For many people, it won't include leading others at all. But at any level, success at work means getting other people to do things with you and for you. And when you face new challenges like these, your instinct might be to focus on learning new skills. But that's only part of the answer. This book is about the other part, the part we wish someone had told us earlier in our careers!

It's not just personal transitions that make conversations matter. Right now, work feels more complex than ever. AI, hybrid work, generational shifts, global teams and constant change all put pressure (and ever-increasing importance) on how you connect, lead and deliver. In a world like this, conversations aren't a *nice-to-have*; they're how you cut through the noise, build trust and make progress. Leadership isn't about having all the answers. It isn't about doing everything yourself. It's about influencing, motivating and moving others to do their best work. That's the transition that each leader faces, again and again, at every stage in their career.

There are, of course, frameworks, techniques and tools you can use to help you do this (there are literally thousands of books written on the skills you need to be a leader). And they have a place – many are brilliant. But alongside thinking about *what* you do, you need to recognise that the way you move others to do great work isn't through theory or a model; it's by connecting and making it easier for people to feel clear, supported and able to perform… and that's through the conversations you have. Every. Single. Day.

This isn't a new idea. Decades of research and writing (much of which we draw on in this book) show that trust, clarity, performance and growth are built through conversation. What's been missing isn't insight; it's integration and breadth. Leadership development has often treated conversations as something that only matters in specific moments: when things go wrong, when performance drops or when we're formally 'coaching'. This book brings the full range of conversations leaders need to have into focus and makes them usable in the everyday moments leaders experience.

Conversations as the catalyst for performance

> 'Performance happens as a result of human connectivity. Human connectivity occurs or fails to occur one conversation at a time.'
>
> – Susan Scott

As Scott sets out in her book *Fierce Conversations* (2017), the conversations we have or don't have either connect or separate us as human beings. That's why conversations are the catalyst for performance. They spark action and accelerate change. Conversations are the bridge between intent and impact: between what you expect and need, and how others respond and what they deliver.

As a leader of people, teams or organisations, you can't do everything yourself. You have to rely on others and support them to deliver what matters. In essence, you need to get others to get stuff done. And the way you do that? You guessed it: through conversations. So, why do conversations matter more than anything you do as a leader? Because they don't just affect you; they shape the experience of your team and, ultimately, your entire organisation.

> Success as a leader comes from your team delivering on its outcomes. The conversations you do (or don't) have move you towards (or away from) these outcomes.

The most common development area we notice across all the work we do is the impact that having (or not having) conversations that matter has on the performance of a team and an organisation as a whole. And when those conversations don't happen, the consequences repeat again and again:

- **unclear expectations:** work isn't delivered as needed or expected
- **avoided feedback:** performance doesn't improve, and standards drop
- **lack of development:** people feel stuck, demotivated and frustrated
- **missed opportunities for connection:** trust erodes and people withdraw.

Left unchecked, these consequences don't disappear; they compound into bigger issues: frustrated teams that people leave, overwhelmed leaders stuck in reactive, firefighting mode or organisations that stall rather than scale.

Conversations don't only happen externally

And even though in this book we're focusing on the conversations you have with others, they always start in your own head: the stories you tell yourself, the assumptions you make, the doubts or confidence you carry into the room. Think of the last time you held back from saying something because you assumed how the other person would react or hesitated about whether it was the right moment. Those inner conversations shape the external ones. Catching and managing them is part of the work of leadership too.

The three levels of impact that conversations can have

Throughout this book, we'll explore how the conversations you have (or don't have) shape success at three levels:

- **for you:** conversations shape your growth, your career and your leadership success. One avoided conversation can stall your progress, erode your confidence or limit your opportunities.
- **for your team:** conversations impact the people you lead. Whether people feel motivated, clear and engaged or frustrated, stuck and second-guessing depends on the quality of the interactions they have with you.

- **for your organisation:** the cumulative effect of conversations creates either a culture of high performance, ownership and trust or one of confusion, low standards and disengagement, ultimately holding the organisation back.

We've seen this play out countless times. In one leadership programme, a senior leader realised they had been avoiding difficult conversations with their team. They prided themselves on being approachable and supportive, but in reality they were skirting around underperformance.

For them personally, this avoidance created frustration; they felt weighed down by issues that never moved forward. For their team, it meant standards were unclear and people were left guessing what was expected. And for the organisation, the impact was tangible: missed deadlines, uneven quality and a culture where *just enough* seemed acceptable.

When the leader made this link and began addressing issues directly, had regular check-ins and gave clear feedback, the shift was immediate. Their own confidence grew, the team stepped up and the organisation saw clear improvement in both delivery and morale. It was the same people, in the same roles, with the same work to do; the difference was the conversations that were now happening.

Conversations are the work of leadership

If you want to be a confident, effective, impactful leader, get better at the conversations that make leadership work. Because without them you stay stuck, and so do the people you lead and work with. And here's a spoiler for later chapters: it isn't about finding the perfect words; it's about creating real human connection – the kind that shifts thinking, strengthens relationships and moves us forward.

So if it's clear that conversations are the work of leadership, then why do so many of us avoid them, rush them or miss the opportunity to have them altogether? That's the question we'll explore next...

Chapter 2

Why great conversations are easy in theory (but hard in practice)

Have you ever told yourself you were going to have a conversation and then, when it came to it, you didn't? Maybe you were all set to give some feedback but, in the moment, hesitated and decided to wait for a better moment. Or you wanted to check in on how someone was getting on with a project but didn't want to seem as if you were micromanaging.

Deep down, you knew what needed to be said, but couldn't get the words out. We've all been there. In theory it's obvious that you need to say what needs to be said. In practice... it's not so simple.

So, what gets in the way of having great conversations?

Much of what we share in this book may feel like common sense. In theory, it's logical: how we interact as humans impacts how we perform. But what's easy in theory is, in our experience, rarely (if ever) practised consistently. Why? These three interlinked dynamics help explain why great conversations don't happen as often, or as effectively as they could.

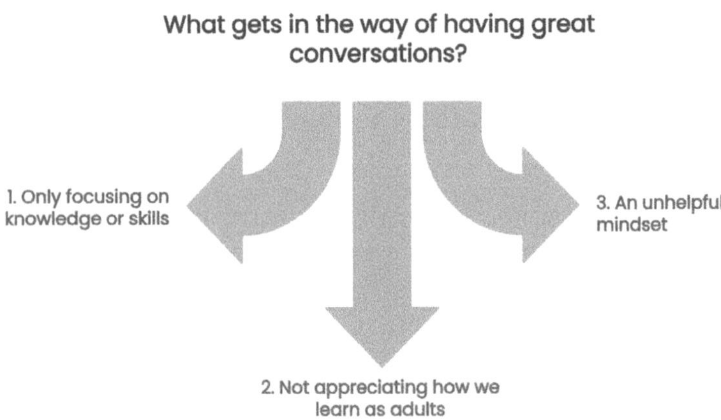

Reason 1: Only focusing on knowledge and skills

As the title of this book suggests, we *will* be giving you a clear framework for understanding the five conversations you need to have at work. When we mention a framework, we know the instinct to skip straight to the theory is strong, the part where you can gain the knowledge that feels actionable right away.

Maybe you're already poised to flip ahead to the chapters where we share practical examples of each conversation. If that's you, and you recognise that pull to go straight to the how-to and skip the background, you're definitely not alone. It's something we've all done when reading a new book. And this takes us directly to the first reason that conversations don't happen consistently.

The challenge: knowledge and skills alone aren't enough. Yet they often get most of the attention in development because they're easier to measure, more tangible and promise quick wins. In your fast-paced workplace, it's natural to focus on learning more or building new skills, thinking that once you know *what* to do, you'll automatically know *how* to do it. The reality? You probably don't, and instead a gap appears between what you know in theory and what you actually do in practice.

As a leader you might know you need to have certain conversations at work, but without paying attention to how you show up and behave in those moments – the *being* part – it just doesn't work. To make these conversations happen consistently, you need to shift from simply knowing *what* needs to be done to consistently putting it into practice, every time.

And sometimes it's not just the external conversation that's missing; it's the inner one too. As leaders, we don't stop to ask ourselves:

> 'Why am I hesitating here?
> What am I avoiding?'

These inner conversations matter. They can either unlock our confidence or reinforce our doubts, and they determine whether we speak up or step back.

All three elements need to be considered for change to happen consistently:

- **Knowing:** gaining knowledge is the first step. It gives you the theoretical understanding and the information you need. But on its own it can be abstract and unused.
- **Doing:** skills allow you to put knowledge into action. They move you from simply understanding what needs to be done to actually knowing how to do it.
- **Being:** is what makes sure knowledge and skills are applied consistently, effectively and (crucially) even when the going gets tough. It's where your inner conversations (the stories you tell yourself, the doubts you manage) meet your actions. Being is all about adapting your behaviours and mindset based on the knowledge and skills you've gained and internalising them so they become a natural part of how you operate.

We will of course come to the *what* and the *how* of each conversation in detail in Chapters 5-9 of this book, and we very much hope to provide enough theory, structure and practical tools to allow you to feel confident to have the conversations that matter. But reading alone won't be enough to make these conversations a consistent part of your approach. Crucially, you must pay attention to the *being* part too. Here are some ways you can start:

- **Be intentional:** set clear goals and be structured and disciplined rather than just *expecting* it to happen. Think about what you're going to commit to both on good days *and* when you're under pressure.
- **Reflect:** take the time to reflect on what you're doing, how you're doing it and the impact it's having. Consider what you are learning and what you need to do differently next time.
- **Get input from others:** be open about what you're trying to do and the areas you'd benefit from having feedback on (for example, your consistency, the impact it's having, what is working, what could be improved).
- **Get support:** peer support is a great way of holding each other to account and learning together. So, find a colleague or friend, buy them this book and support each other to make the shifts needed.
- **Learn from others:** identify role models or colleagues who do some of the things you're trying to do and ask what helps them.

Reason 2: Not appreciating how we learn as adults

Understanding how adults learn is crucial for applying any new knowledge, skills or behaviour to have great conversations at work. Adult development theory or, as Alis Anagnostakis (founder of the Vertical Development Institute) calls it, *how grown-ups grow up,* is based on the theory that as an adult you learn from, and operate across, a number of *vertical development levels*.

You move through these levels when you realise that to overcome a challenge or seize an opportunity, you need to think and act differently. Your movement across the levels is not linear and personal growth cannot be achieved simply by racing to the most mature stage of development. You need to use all levels in a thorough and dynamic way, learning lessons from each level. This is where experiences come in.

Every experience you have, whether it's at work or in your personal life, offers an opportunity to grow. What you learn from how you approach each experience, the impact it had on you and others, and what you take forward from that learning is what helps you to develop.

Such experiences could be:

- dealing with a disgruntled customer in your first holiday job in a bar
- failing your first attempt at your driving test
- being given your first project to manage on your own

- winning an employee of the month award
- being asked to manage someone else for the first time
- navigating your first heartbreak
- getting some difficult feedback on a piece of work
- being left out of a group or team you wanted to be part of
- making a big mistake at work and having to fix it
- achieving something you didn't think you could
- missing out on a role or promotion you thought you'd get.

When we work as coaches and facilitators for leadership development, we see first hand how adults experience both horizontal (skills-based) and vertical (mindset and perspective-based) development.

Real transformation happens when people are pushed outside their comfort zone: when they begin to experience what's called *conscious incompetence*. This is the moment when you realise there's a gap between what you know and what you're (currently) capable of, and it's uncomfortable but necessary. Seeing that gap takes deep self-awareness: a mix of internal reflection (what you know about yourself) and external feedback (what others help you to see).

The Conscious Competence Ladder, developed by Noel Burch in the 1970s, illustrates how we move from being unaware of our *incompetence* to achieving *conscious competence* in new skills, which for us in this book is how to have great conversations. This model highlights the importance of reflection in making progress. And of facilitated reflection, where someone helps you to look at your experiences from a new angle, is often one of the greatest enablers of transformational development.

The Conscious Competence Ladder

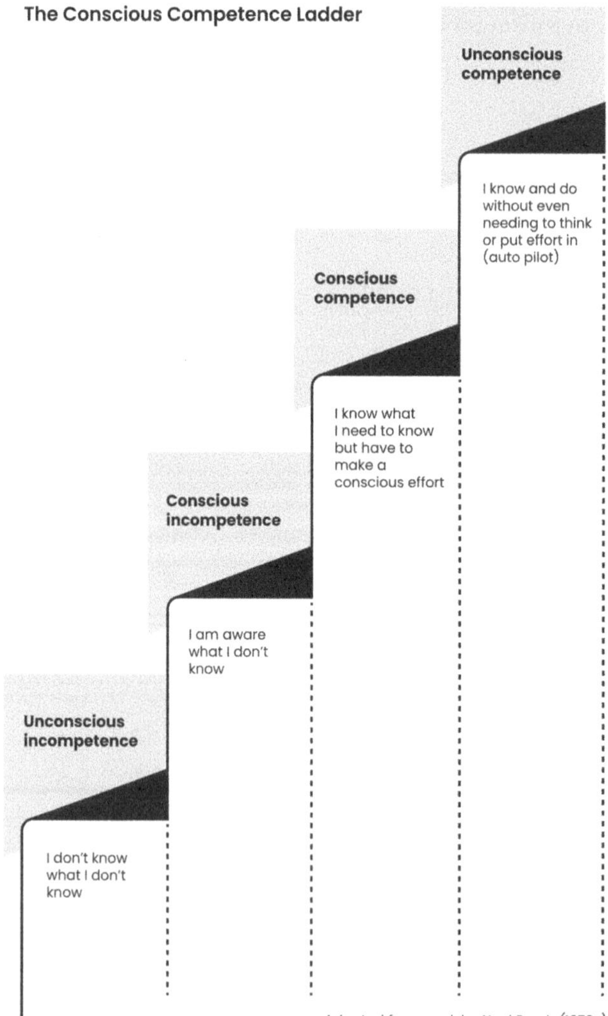

Adapted from work by Noel Burch (1970s)

High-performing, happy, successful individuals and leaders find ways to continually raise their self-awareness, find their *gap*, reflect and take action. Put simply, learning often starts with a moment of tension, that discomfort, when we pause and think:

'I'm not sure I know how to do this...'

or

'I've not done this before...'

It's in this space, in this conversation with ourselves, where growth can start to happen, but only if we choose to listen, reflect and act. Conversations, like any skill, provide opportunities for learning. But only if you approach them intentionally. And it's not just about your own growth. As a leader, one of the most powerful things you can do is to help others to learn and grow. Conversations are how we can create the space for that to happen, but again, only if we do it intentionally. Here are some ways you can use conversations to help others make the most of learning opportunities.

- **Create a safe space for discomfort:** for example, 'I know this might feel a bit tricky, I want to support you' or 'I'm pausing to give you time to think, not because I expect a certain answer.'
- **Encourage reflection:** help the other person dig into the learning, for example by asking, 'What did you learn as part of X? What impact will that learning have for you in the future?'

- **Give constructive feedback with areas for growth:** add a stretch with something like, 'One thing that could make this even stronger is...' We'll go into this in much more depth in Chapter 8.
- **Make experimentation possible:** encourage the other person to try something new by explicitly opening up the opportunity for experimentation. For example, you might say: 'It's OK if this doesn't go as planned; we'll learn from it either way.' This approach helps them embrace the process and understand that mistakes are part of growth, and fosters a mindset of learning through trial and error.
- **Share your own experiences:** open up about your own learning to create connection and trust. For example, you could say, 'I've faced something similar before, and here's what I learned from it.' This helps to normalise the learning process, shows vulnerability and encourages openness and shared growth.

Reason 3: An unhelpful mindset

> '...as you begin to understand... mindsets, you will see exactly how one thing leads to another, how a belief that your qualities are carved in stone leads to a host of thoughts and actions, and how a belief that your qualities can be cultivated leads to a host of different thoughts and actions, taking you down an entirely different road.'
>
> – Carol Dweck, *Mindset: The New Psychology of Success* (2006)

Your mindset is a unique and deeply ingrained set of beliefs that shape how you interpret the world and your place in it. It goes beyond how you feel in any given moment; it directly impacts how you think, the actions you take and how you engage with others. Think of mindset as the filter through which you view each situation, especially in challenging moments, influencing your responses during conversations.

These beliefs don't just appear. They're formed over time, shaped by experiences, influences and the interpretations you've made along the way. They can be helpful or unhelpful, positive or negative, and they often operate on autopilot, without you realising how much they affect your actions.

You might see a connection here to unconscious bias (or implicit bias), the automatic judgements people make about others based on past experiences and assumptions.

The term unconscious bias was introduced in the 1990s by psychologists Mahzarin Banaji and

Anthony Greenwald, who showed that our social behaviour is often shaped by unconscious associations. These automatic mental shortcuts help us to make quick decisions, but they can also influence our thinking and in turn the actions we take, without us even realising it.

And just like bias, mindsets form in similar ways: shaped by your experiences, repeated patterns and interpretations that run in the background unless you pause to notice and examine them.

The link between mindset and conversations

Think about something that's happened today, at work or at home. Which beliefs were guiding your thoughts and actions in that moment? Were they helpful and productive, or did they get in your way? When you start noticing those beliefs, especially in challenging moments, you can get a clearer sense of your mindset. And it's this mindset that shapes the actions you take and the results you get.

When you hold limiting beliefs about yourself, others or the situation in front of you, they can shape the way you approach a conversation. Take a leadership example: if you believe 'I need to have all the answers' it might stop you from adopting a *coaching approach* in problem-solving conversations (we'll explore this in detail in Chapters 4 and 9). Rather than guiding others to find their own solutions, you might jump straight in to *fix* the issue yourself, stifling collaboration and growth.

These moments often start with quiet, internal chatter:

> 'What if I say the wrong thing? What if I make it worse? What if they don't take me seriously?'

Recognising these thoughts as just that, thoughts not facts, is the first step to choosing a more helpful mindset.

Let's explore this in practice.

Naomi writes: About five years into my leadership career, I hired someone with more experience than I had in certain areas. A small seed of unease grew as the new hire's first day approached. I recall how I felt before the first one-to-one: nervous, unsure of how to approach the meeting.

Here are some of the beliefs that shaped my mindset at the time:

- I wouldn't know how to support their development.
- They couldn't possibly learn anything from me.
- They would think they should be doing my role.
- They would become frustrated and disengaged and decide they'd made a mistake taking the job.

If left unchecked, these beliefs could have affected how I handled the first conversation, creating a barrier to connection and collaboration. But by pausing to reflect on my mindset, I was able challenge those beliefs and shift my approach. How? As we now do with all our clients, I asked myself, 'What does good look like here for both of us?' My answer was that we would get to know each other better, understand how we each liked to work and figure out how we could bring out the best in one another. So, I took this learning into the conversation and was open about what I had been thinking. I asked questions such as:

- 'I'm impressed by the breadth and depth of your skills and experience and I'm wondering how I can support your ongoing development?'
- 'I know you've had many different team experiences. What can you share about what works and doesn't work for you?'
- 'I'm sure there's a lot we can learn from you as well. What would make it comfortable for you to share areas where you think we can improve?'

The result? My honesty encouraged my new colleague to do the same. They admitted they were nervous about working in a new sector and that, when they feel nervous, they sometimes struggle to recognise their own contributions. They also shared that small talk doesn't come easy to them and they'd appreciate me drawing them into conversations and making key introductions.

By putting these potential barriers out there, I established a foundation of openness from the start. Mindset played a crucial role in how I approached the conversation, and this shift led to better results.

Great conversations start with mindset. Notice it, nurture it and it'll shape the results you get *and* the way people experience working with you.

In summary

As we've explored in this chapter, having great conversations at work sounds simple in theory. You know what needs to be said and you may even have the skills to say it. But the challenge is doing it consistently. That needs more than knowledge. It requires reflection, mindset shifts and behavioural change. As adults, we often focus on gaining knowledge and skills, but real growth comes from reflecting on how you apply them and adapting your approach in each situation.

You don't just need to know *what* to do. You need to do things differently, even when it's uncomfortable or easier not to. That means paying attention not just to the conversations you have with others, but also to the ones you have with yourself.

When you bring together knowing, doing and being, and pay attention to the mindset behind your actions, you give yourself a better chance of turning good intentions into lasting habits.

And that's what makes the difference.

If you remember only one thing:

Knowing what to say isn't enough. How you approach the conversation and what you believe about it will shape how it's received.

Chapter 3

The five conversations that change everything

At work, you're talking to people all the time: in meetings, over coffee, on virtual calls, at your desk, at lunch. Most of these conversations happen without much thought. But not all of them move you towards the outcomes that matter. Some build trust, clarify priorities and make progress. Others waste time, cause frustration or add confusion. The real question isn't whether you're having conversations – it's whether you're having the right ones, intentionally.

By now you'll see why conversations are so important at work. But while you know they matter, putting them into practice consistently is another challenge. In our experience, there isn't a single *magic conversation* that fixes everything. What matters is having the right kinds of conversations again and again: ones that foster connection, create clarity, support development, improve performance and solve problems.

And it's not about saving everything up for a big formal meeting. The most powerful conversations at work are short, informal and unplanned. A five-minute check-in, a quick reset or a moment of reflection together. These moments build momentum, create habits and make conversations feel more natural and less *heavy* or onerous.

> **Consistency beats perfection.** Leadership isn't about one big conversation; it's about all the little ones that come before it.

When conversations don't happen, things start to unravel. Slowly at first, almost invisibly, but they unravel all the same. A team that looks good on paper starts missing deadlines, but no one calls it out or talks about why. Frustrations grow but feedback isn't given. Performance dips further. Priorities and expectations aren't clear, so team members work on what feels important *to them*. There's no time for personal or team development, ambition and energy start to fade and eventually good people leave. There's no single moment you can point to, no dramatic event, just a leader left wondering, 'How did things get to this?'

That's why having conversations, and having them often, matters.

Introducing the five conversations

Since we promised you a framework, let's deliver on that now. We've identified five key types of workplace conversations that, when done well, help individuals and teams thrive:

- **Conversations for connection**: building relationships so that every other conversation is easier and more impactful.
- **Conversations for clarity and alignment**: ensuring shared understanding and expectations so that everyone is working towards the same goals.
- **Conversations for development**: helping people learn, stretch and make progress in their skills, confidence and careers.
- **Conversations for performance improvement**: addressing challenges early so that small issues don't turn into bigger problems.
- **Conversations for problem solving**: overcoming challenges and uncertainties together.

These aren't rigid, stand-alone conversations that happen in isolation. In reality, a single conversation might touch on all five types: you might check in with someone (**connection**), clarify expectations (**clarity and alignment**), explore future opportunities (**development**), give feedback (**performance improvement**) and collaborate on a solution (**problem solving**), all in the same discussion.

The five conversations

Conversation	Includes	Key impacts
Conversations for connection	Informal interactions, quick check ins, appreciation and positive feedback	Ensures people feel connected, valued, cared about and builds trust
Conversations for clarity and alignment	Setting goals, delegating or starting new pieces of work and ongoing progress and priority discussions	Creates stability, agility, alignment and identifies issues early
Conversations for development	Explore aspirations and development areas. Space to reflect on learning	Develops, highlights strengths and performance, engages motivates, retains
Conversations for performance improvement	Constructive, timely and specific positive and improvement feedback	Addresses performance issues, raises awareness, develops, reiterates expectations
Conversations for problem solving	Resolving challenges and overcoming barriers and blockers	Avoids delays and bigger issues arising, and keeps ownership where it needs to be

So, rather than thinking of these as five separate conversations you need to plan for, think of them as the five things that most need to be talked about across all of your interactions. When these conversations aren't happening regularly, things start to unravel, misalignment grows, frustration builds and opportunities are missed.

These five conversations aren't a step-by-step process or a rigid framework. They're the core workplace conversations that make the biggest difference.

We'll explore each one in depth in the chapters ahead, but for now, here's a brief overview of what they're all about.

Conversations for connection

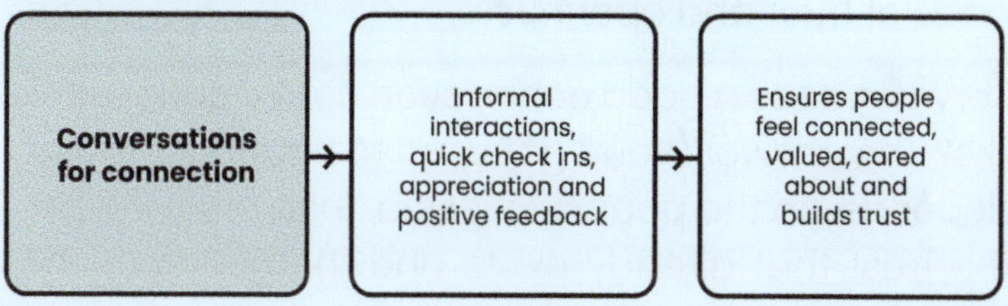

Think about the best leader or manager you've ever had. What made them stand out? Chances are it wasn't how much they knew, it was how they made you feel. They probably made you feel valued, important, and they took the time to understand you as a person. This is what conversations for connection are all about. These are the conversations that lay the foundation for everything else.

Yet, despite their importance, conversations for connection often get put into the 'too fluffy' category or the 'Is just a chat a good use of time?' category, rather than being treated as a priority. You might find yourself thinking you're too busy or that small talk doesn't feel necessary. And when you do have those catch-ups, it's easy not to give them the quality of attention they deserve.

> Conversations for connection aren't about small talk.

Conversations for connection are about strengthening relationships so that, when the bigger conversations need to happen, they happen on a basis of trust and openness.

So, what does a good connection conversation look like? The answer (you'll get used to hearing this) is it depends: on the people involved, their preferences, the trust that already exists and the needs of the two people involved in the conversation.

Unlike the other conversations in this book, which often have a specific topic for discussion, the best conversations for connection happen when there isn't a defined agenda. They create a space to connect, to reflect, to check in and to talk about more than just tasks.

Here are some ways to approach conversations for connection:

- **Consciously shift your mindset** from 'Do I have time for this?' to 'What impact could this have?' Connection isn't a distraction from work; it's the foundation for better work.
- **Be fully present:** the quality of your attention matters more than the quantity of time you give.
- **Approach with curiosity:** notice any assumptions you might be making and let them go. Instead, genuinely seek to understand the other person's perspective.

These conversations build trust, belonging and collaboration. They're not just about being friendly, they're how we build strong *human* relationships – the ones that make work happen.

> When people feel seen, heard, valued and cared about, everything else becomes possible.

And if you're still in the 'I'm not convinced this is a good use of time' camp, keep reading, we promise we'll help you change your mind.

Conversations for clarity and alignment

We've all left a meeting thinking that everyone is aligned on what needs to be done, only to realise later that there have been different interpretations of what was said. Maybe the update you expected to receive didn't happen or the output delivered wasn't what you needed.

Clarity and alignment conversations bring direction and focus to the workplace. Without them, confusion, misalignment, frustration, stress and wasted effort can creep in, making it harder for people to do their best work. With these conversations teams move faster and more confidently. They collaborate better and can adapt to changes more easily too. Yet, these conversations are often rushed or assumed to have happened when, in reality, they haven't. As this widely used phrase goes:

> 'The single biggest problem in communication is the illusion that it has taken place.'

Sometimes you might assume these conversations aren't needed because everything feels clear... at least in your own head. But they're essential to set out and continue to be aligned on priorities, objectives, understanding, values, expectations and timelines. You name it, whatever matters to delivering outcomes needs to be talked about regularly.

So, what does good look like? Once again, it depends. This time, on the complexity of the work, the experience level of the people involved and how often things change. What's certain is that these conversations are most effective when they're intentional, ongoing and involve genuine two-way dialogue, not just top-down instructions.

Some ways to approach conversations for clarity and alignment:

- **Be explicit and check for understanding.** Clarity isn't about what you said; it's about what was heard and understood.
- **Treat alignment as an ongoing conversation.** Not a one-off agreement. The best teams don't just align once; they check in, adjust and recalibrate as things evolve.
- **Balance precision with flexibility.** It's not about rigid control; it's about giving people the confidence to move forward.

These conversations stop people heading off in different directions. They remove assumptions, clear up confusion and create a shared view of what good looks like. And they make work feel better by reducing friction, increasing focus and helping teams perform at their best.

If you've ever felt like you're working hard but not quite moving in the right direction, or not moving quickly enough, Chapter 6 will help you see why and how to fix it.

Conversations for development

Think about your team right now. Does everyone seem equally engaged? Maybe someone's doing what they need to, but they seem distracted or disconnected. Or maybe someone has lost their mojo or wants to be promoted but there aren't any roles available, so you're reluctant to ask them about it in case it makes things worse. This is where conversations for development come in.

These are the conversations that help people grow, stretch and see a future beyond their current role. And they're not just about promotions or formal career plans. They're about helping people feel valued, challenged and motivated, and they can happen in everyday interactions, not just in annual development reviews.

Without them, people can feel stuck, stagnant, undervalued or unsure about what's next. And yet, these conversations often get overlooked in the busyness of day-to-day work. You might assume development will happen naturally, or that it only needs to be discussed in formal reviews. But real development is nurtured in small, everyday conversations.

These conversations don't just help people grow in their careers; they help them feel seen, valued and inspired to do their best work. So, what does good look like? Unsurprisingly, it depends. This time, it depends on the individual and their aspirations, motivations and personal context.

Unlike performance discussions, which focus on the here and now, development conversations look ahead. They explore possibilities and build confidence by helping people see their own potential. They require curiosity and for us to let go of assumptions about what someone wants.

> Conversations for development are about the person as well as the organisation. It's not just *what they need to develop*, it's also about *what they want to achieve for themselves.*

Here are some ways to approach conversations for development:

- **Let go of your version of what career success looks like.** Sometimes it's less about 'What next?' and more about 'What excites you?' Development doesn't have to be about moving up; it's as much about understanding what keeps people engaged and fulfilled at work.

- **Hold the need to solve lightly.** The best development conversations don't give answers or even result in solid actions; they give people the space to explore and uncover what matters most to them.
- **Be open to possibilities, not just plans.** Career paths aren't always linear, and development can take lots of forms.

These conversations are about growth and long-term performance. They go beyond job titles and promotions; they help people reflect, learn and stretch. They're the conversations that help build confidence, direction, motivation and capability.

If you've ever wondered 'What's next for me?' or struggled to support someone else in answering that question, Chapter 7 will help.

Conversations for performance improvement

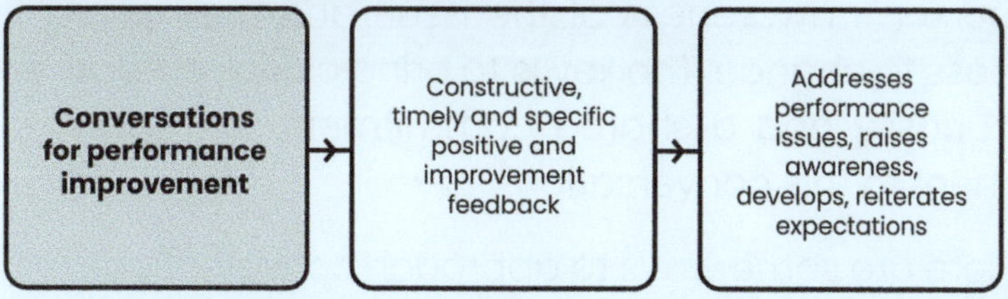

Think about those times when you've spotted the early signs of a performance issue. Maybe someone missed a deadline, delivered below expectations or their behaviour started to affect others. Did you address it straight away? Or did you hesitate, talk yourself out of it, not wanting to make the situation worse? Did you hope it was just a blip that would resolve itself on its own?

Performance improvement conversations are the ones that help people get back on track, improve their effectiveness and ultimately succeed in their roles. Without them, small issues become bigger problems. Frustration builds, performance dips further and both individuals and teams suffer.

Yet these conversations are often the ones people put off the most. Maybe you're worried about damaging relationships, you feel awkward or you simply don't know how to begin. Deep down you know that avoiding these conversations doesn't help; it only makes things harder later. When handled well, conversations for performance improvement aren't about criticism – they're about balancing challenge with support and working together to get things back on track.

So, what does good look like? You guessed it – it depends. This time, it depends on the situation, the person's awareness of the issue and their willingness to change. The key is to bring clarity, empathy, curiosity and a shared commitment to improvement to this conversation.

Here are some ways to approach conversations for performance improvement:

- **Be curious, not certain.** Avoid making assumptions about the person's abilities, decisions and behaviours. They may not be true.
- **Choose honesty over harmony.** Being nice avoids the issue; being kind means having it *and* approaching it with care.
- **Prioritise the conversation over the script.** What you say matters far less than the conversation that it opens up between the two of you.

These conversations are the tools you have for getting things back on track when something's off and before it becomes a bigger issue. They're not about blame and you don't need to have all the answers to begin.

> Performance improvement conversations are about bringing something to the table for discussion and standing side by side to look at it together.

If you've ever struggled to deliver tough feedback or worried about how to start a difficult performance conversation, Chapter 8 will give you the tools and confidence to do it well.

Conversations for problem solving

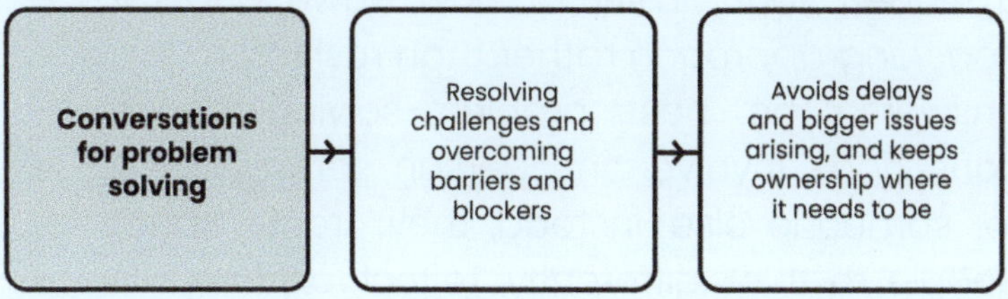

And finally, let's talk about conversations for problem solving.

How often do you feel frustrated when someone brings you problems rather than solutions? How often do you feel as if you're holding all the responsibility, involved in every decision, constantly firefighting and fixing, leaving little time for the work you need to focus on?

Problem-solving conversations are the ones that help you navigate challenges, overcome roadblocks and move forward. Without them your team can get stuck in frustration, inefficiency or blame, instead of working together to solve what's in front of them. The irony? You might avoid these conversations because they feel uncomfortable, because you're unsure how to ask the right questions or because it's easier to just fix the problem yourself.

As leaders, we often fall into the trap of jumping in to fix things. It's so easy (and even validating) to offer quick answers. But these conversations offer a better option, one where you support others to take ownership, instead of relying on you to solve it all.

So, what does good look like? You guessed it – it depends. This time, it depends on the complexity of the problem, who's involved and, crucially as a leader, your ability to slow down and take a *coaching approach* rather than rushing to provide answers. The best problem-solving conversations don't involve one person solving the issue for someone else. Instead, they create space for people to think differently, reflect, explore options and take ownership.

Here are some ways to approach conversations for problem solving:

- **Get clear on the problem you're actually solving.** If someone asked, would you both explain it in the same way?
- **Reframe how you add value.** Offering solutions isn't the only way (or often the best way) to help.
- **Watch for the hot potato.** Who's holding it right now? (Intrigued? You'll have to read Chapter 4 to find out more).

These conversations create something you often lack: space. Space to think through what's happening, what's needed and what's next.

> Conversations for problem solving aren't about having all the answers; they're about helping people get unstuck. And in doing so, helping them realise they're capable of more than they thought.

If you've ever felt as if you need to have all the answers or found yourself frustrated that people keep bringing you problems, Chapter 9 will help you shift your approach.

So, conversations matter – a lot! A great conversation could strengthen a relationship, build trust, drive performance and even be the reason a talented member of your team chooses to stay and go the extra mile instead of looking for a job elsewhere. **When you think about it that way, could it actually be the most impactful thing you can do today?**

But... as we discussed in Chapter 2, knowing that conversations matter isn't enough. It's about how we approach them that makes the difference. So, how do you turn an ordinary conversation into a great one? And how do you have more of them?

Let's explore that next...

Chapter 4

What makes a conversation great?

How do we make the leap from theory to action? And how do we know which conversation to have?

A useful way of thinking about this came to us through a leadership team workshop we facilitated. One participant could understand the theory in principle but was stuck on *knowing* what type of conversation to have, and it was getting in the way of him being able to put it into practice.

Rather than pretending he understood and going through the motions in the workshop exercises we had planned, he told us in no uncertain terms that it wasn't going to work for him if he couldn't see how he could apply it. Through him asking the question to make sense for himself, we also found the way we now frame this for others, so thank you, AJ, for your persistence!

Imagine for a moment you have fallen, your wrist is swollen and you're in significant pain. If it's broken, you'll need to have a cast or at least a sling. If it's just a sprain, then rest and painkillers will do the trick. So, you go to A&E to find out. When you arrive at A&E, doctors don't jump immediately to diagnosis, and this is where the medical world and the leadership world align. To be able to define accurately the best response, they *triage* first: assessing before deciding on treatment.

Even if you had just badly bruised or cut your wrist, the response wouldn't be decided until the extent, scale and specific nature of the injury had been assessed. And the same goes for conversations. Even if on the surface what is needed appears obvious, you need to refrain from jumping to conclusions and instead ask a couple of questions to determine (in essence triage) the situation. Doing this with your colleagues allows you to work *with them* to determine the best conversation to move you both forward. There will be more to come on what this means in practice later in this chapter.

As we touched on in the last chapter, these conversations don't need to be long or formal to be effective. The more regularly you have them, in all their imperfect, in-the-moment, human forms, the easier it gets to have them and to notice what's needed. And the more comfortable *others* feel having them too.

And that's what this chapter is all about: the practical side of making conversations great, when to ask and when to tell, where responsibility should sit and how to listen well.

Listen up

To be able to triage effectively, you need to listen. Not just *hear* the words being said but *listen* in a way that helps you figure out what's really going on.

The problem is that most of us don't listen in this way. We listen with half our attention, already preparing what we're going to say next in our head before the other person has even finished speaking – waiting for a pause to jump in. We listen to *fix* rather than to *understand*. But if you want to have better conversations, you need to get better at choosing the right conversation, and listening is the only way you'll do this. In practice this means things such as:

- stopping yourself when you want to jump in – try leaving some silence instead
- getting curious, even if you think you know what's going on. You aren't in the other person's head, so you can't be certain – ask some open questions to let them share more about what is going on for them
- checking your understanding by playing back what you've heard.

Without this kind of listening, you risk misdiagnosing. This might be offering advice when someone just wants to share what they're thinking or jumping to an action plan when what they actually want is reassurance.

What happens in a conversation

Beyond listening and choosing the right conversation, you also need to think about what you actually *do* in the conversation itself.

To help you to think about this, we want to introduce you to the conversation spectrum. Put simply, this is a common way of setting out what happens in *coaching-style* conversations and was represented visually by Myles Downing to do just that in his book *Effective Modern Coaching: The principles and art of successful business coaching* (2014).

We have adapted it and expanded its use, and for us it serves as a visual way to represent the range of *all the things* that can happen, in *all* conversations.

At one end of the spectrum, you *ask* and at the other, you *tell*. If you've used a *coaching style* before you might recognise these as *non-directive* and *directive*. Or, often the distinction given to explain the difference between coaching and mentoring.

When delivering workshops, we often spend more time looking at how to bring aspects of *asking* or being *non-directive* into conversations. That's not because this end of the spectrum is more important, but because, for most of us, it goes against our default (very human) instinct to give advice. You could say our directive conversation muscle is often very well toned!

Image (opposite) adapted from work by Myles Downing

What makes a conversation great?

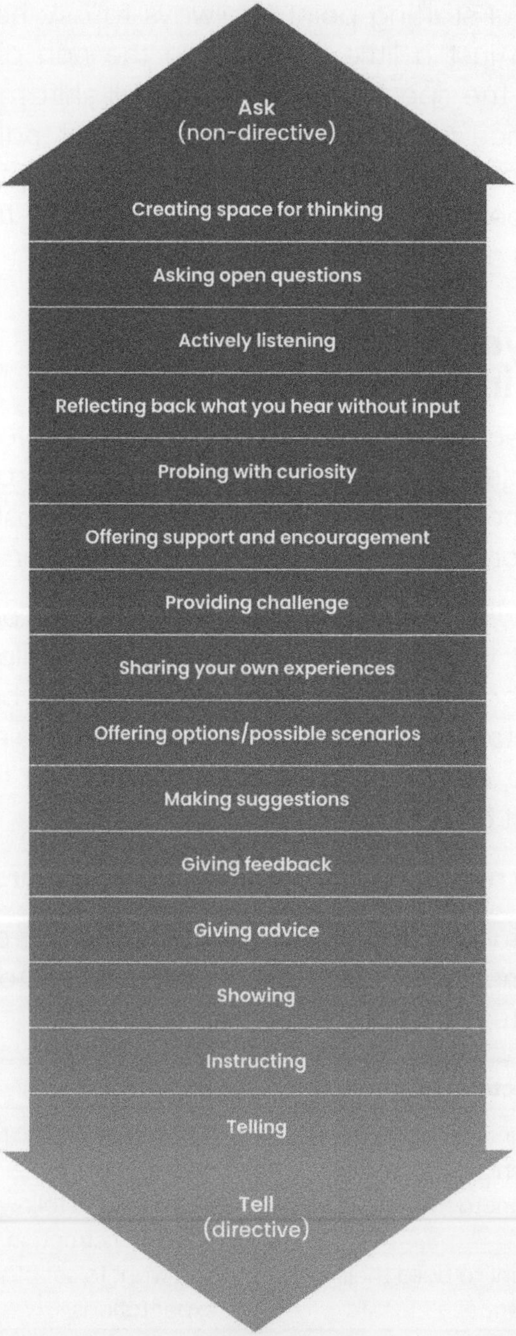

A helpful starting point is always to ask: how can you do just a little bit more in the non-directive end of the spectrum? Even a small shift makes a difference. And, of course, the flip side of that is that sometimes being non-directive isn't helpful. The key is being able to move fluidly between the two, up and down the spectrum as needed.

How you decide what to do in a conversation

The spectrum shows the range of options you have available in any conversation. As with many aspects of this book, there isn't a binary answer: most situations don't fit neatly at one end or the other.

For now, however, here are some questions you can ask yourself and some examples to help you to think about where on the spectrum might be most useful to start. Of course, some of these factors overlap, or are combined with others, but for now let's just think about what they are.

1. What am I trying to achieve in the conversation?

A helpful starting point is to define what a good outcome for the conversation looks like, or what your intention is, for example:

Non-directive if...	**Directive if...**
➤ You want them to take ownership. ➤ You want to hear their ideas. ➤ You want to build their confidence.	➤ You need to deliver a clear message. ➤ They need to follow a specific instruction. ➤ You want to set clear expectations.

2. Who is bringing the topic for discussion?

We often use the term *gap* here. By that we mean that there is:

- a gap between where someone is and where they need to be
- a gap between what is happening and what needs to happen
- a gap between what they want and what they're doing
- a gap between their intention and their impact
- a gap between how they see things and how others see them
- a gap between effort and outcome
- a gap between understanding and action.

So, the key question here is: who's already aware of the gap? If *they're* bringing the topic (or concern, challenge or idea), they're likely already aware of the gap that exists between where they are now and where they want or need to be.

If *you're* bringing the topic, your aim is to help them see, acknowledge or understand that gap, whether it's a gap in performance, standards, expectations or understanding. So this looks like:

Non-directive if...	Directive if...
➤ They're bringing the topic for discussion. ➤ They are seeking help or support or are feeling stuck, showing that they know something isn't working and a gap exists between where they are and where they want to be.	➤ You have identified a gap they don't yet see, whether it's a gap in performance, standards, expectation or understanding. ➤ You need to make the gap visible and explicit for them, because without that awareness nothing will change.

3. How experienced, capable or resourceful is my colleague?

This is all about considering how much experience or knowledge the person already has that they can draw on. Even if they haven't faced this exact situation before, do they have prior learning or experience they can use here? For example:

Non-directive if...	Directive if...
➤ They *have* prior experience, knowledge, skills or learning that they can apply (even if not directly related).	➤ They are facing something genuinely new, with no relevant experience or learning to use, so they need guidance to get started.

4. What is the most helpful role for me to take?

Considering some of the aspects we have already discussed help here, but by *role* some of the things we mean are:

- Is my role to mentor (share my experience)?
- Is my role to facilitate (to enable the thinking to happen)?
- Is my role to challenge (to push someone further than they might push themselves)?

We can't list out all the possible roles you could take, and we might use labels that don't feel like the ones you would use. The key thing, however, is to be intentional about the role that is helpful. And, of course, that isn't just for you to decide. It's completely OK (if not, in fact, hugely useful) to ask the person you're having the conversation with a question such as:

- What role would be most helpful for me to take here?
- What do you need most from me?
- Or another version with words that feel more natural for you.

Try it – you might be surprised that they know the answer!

5. Where does responsibility need to sit?

We get some strange looks when we first introduce the concept of the *hot potato* in workshops. But for us it's one of the best ways to visualise responsibility as a *tangible thing*.

Naomi writes: The origins of the concept are slightly unclear, apart from a hazy memory I have from the school playground. The idea was something along the lines of this: a group of children throw a ball between themselves, wanting to get rid of it as soon as they catch it, as if it's a hot potato straight from the oven that's too hot to hold. The child left holding it at the end of the game loses (the factors that lead to the end of the game is where it gets a little fuzzy…).

So, if we go back to responsibility, at any point in time in a conversation, one of you will hold the responsibility. There will be times when you pass it between you consciously or subconsciously, and times when it might sit between or in front of both of you.

The key is to think about where responsibility needs to sit by reflecting on:

- Who owns the problem?
- Who is responsible for solving it?
- Who will be delivering the solution or doing whatever needs to happen next?

Let's think about an example: a colleague comes to you with a problem on a project they're responsible for delivering.

Your colleague: 'We're going to overrun, and the client isn't going to be happy. What should I do?'

They had the potato (they're holding the problem) and they've thrown it to you by asking you what they should do. You now have two choices, and thinking about responsibility helps you to make that choice intentionally.

Choice 1: you go into *fix* mode and tell them what they should do.

Choice 2: you help them to think it through and work out what to do next, for example:

You: 'OK, so what are your options?'

In choice 1, you keep hold of the potato, and in choice 2, you pass the potato right back to them.

This can carry on throughout the conversation, and at times it might be completely appropriate for you to hold the potato for some of the time. For example, you might have had a previous experience of working with this client that would be useful to share, and you take hold of the potato for a short period before passing it back.

What is key here is that you know when you're holding responsibility and are choosing to do it intentionally.

6. What might I *not* be doing because it feels uncomfortable (for me or them)?

This takes us back to some of the elements we discussed in Chapter 2. As we wrote there, discomfort is a normal part of learning or trying something different (although we get that knowing something is going to be uncomfortable doesn't make it immediately comfortable).

Beliefs you might be holding or what you assume about the other person, such as inferring meaning from body language, predicting how they'll respond to silence or guessing what they're thinking, are all just that: assumptions, until you ask.

And if asking feels uncomfortable, being clear and explicit about your intentions can ease some of that discomfort. For example, you might say:

- 'I'm not trying to make you uncomfortable; I just want to give you a moment to think.'
- 'That's a big question, isn't it? I don't expect you to have an answer immediately. Why don't we explore it together?'

A reminder about fluidity in conversations (or in other words, flexing across the spectrum)

As we said earlier in this chapter, these questions are just a guide. In practice, it's rare for a conversation to sit entirely at one end of the spectrum. For example, you might:

- start with questions, then also offer some guidance or suggestions, or
- give feedback, then help the other person reflect on what it means for them by asking questions.

Shifting from non-directive to directive or vice versa isn't a mistake; it's often a sign of a great conversation. You're responding to what's needed in the moment. The goal isn't to stick rigidly to one end of the spectrum but to move intentionally, based on the situation, the individual and the outcome you're both aiming for. You might hold the responsibility for a moment (hot potato firmly in hand), then pass it back. That's OK – what matters is that you're aware of when and why you're doing it.

If you're not sure where to start, ask yourself: 'What's one small way I can do a little bit more at the non-directive end of the spectrum?'

Because this is the end that often feels less instinctive, for all the reasons we explored earlier in this chapter.

Let's look at what this fluidity might look like in practice with a few examples:

Scenario	**Description**	**Position on the spectrum**
Project delays (conversation for problem solving)	There are delays on a project and you start by asking your colleague what might be causing them.	Non-directive
	They still seem stuck, and you know it's the first time they've dealt with a project like this, so you offer a few observations based on your own experience to help them see options they haven't considered.	Directive
	You then ask them which of the options might be relevant to them right now and what they might want to do next.	Non-directive
Feedback (conversation for performance improvement)	You give some clear feedback on a missed deadline.	Directive
	Rather than assuming you know why it's happened, you create some space to explore what might stop it happening again: 'What would help to avoid this next time?'	Non-directive

Personal development (conversation for development)	You ask a team member what their next development focus should be. They're not sure or give vague examples.	Non-directive
	You offer: 'Would it help if I shared some areas that I think could stretch you from what I have noticed?'	Directive
	You ask them for their reflections on what you have said and which things they might want to consider working on.	Non-directive
Project issue (conversation for problem solving)	You're in a hurry and so when you see an issue, you immediately share what your colleague needs to do to resolve it.	Directive
	But partway through you catch yourself and say: 'I've gone straight into solution mode, haven't I! What are you thinking so far?'	Non-directive
	They share an idea that is even better, and you help them explore what they need to do to take it forward.	Non-directive

Priorities (conversation for clarity and alignment)	You're in a one-to-one, helping your colleague get clear on their priorities for the month. They list everything they feel they need to achieve.	Non-directive
	You share your thoughts: that this is a long list, and perhaps not as focused as it could be on what is most important for their role.	Directive
	They acknowledge this and admit to feeling a bit overwhelmed.	Non-directive
	You suggest that you explore together how to make the list a bit more focused and realistic.	Directive
	You start by asking them: 'What tasks can only you do?'	Non-directive
Disengaged colleague (conversation for connection)	You notice a team member has been a bit quieter than usual in meetings. You share what you have noticed and ask them if there's anything you can help with.	Directive
	They share that they're feeling a bit sidelined. Rather than jumping in with suggestions, you listen, reassure them you're there to support and ask questions that help them explore the situation and identify what steps they can take to improve it.	Non-directive

What else matters in conversations?

If these are the conversations that matter, then how you show up matters just as much. These four Cs create the conditions for conversations to be meaningful and effective – not just in theory but with real humans, in real working relationships.

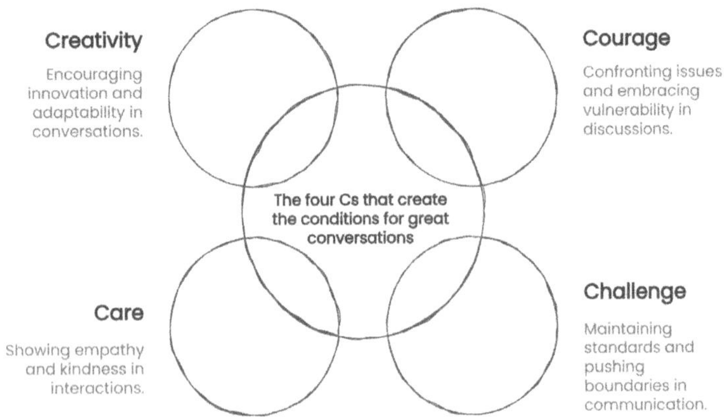

Creativity by:

- **trying** different approaches
- **encouraging** new ideas and being open to them
- **adapting** your style
- **avoiding** the default to what works for you; every person is different
- **recognising** that creativity can take many different forms.

Courage to:

- **confront** issues head on, rather than shying away from having difficult conversations
- **enter** into conversations without knowing what the outcome will be
- **leave** pauses and silence and sit with discomfort
- **admit** when you got it wrong and allow yourself to be vulnerable
- **be open** to learning and asking for feedback.

Challenge by:

- **saying** what needs to be said, when it needs to be said
- **maintaining** standards consistently
- **nipping** things in the bud early
- **refusing** to settle for less than what's needed or expected (if you have made that clear, more on this in Chapter 6)
- **pushing** outside of your comfort zone too.

Caring by:

- **caring** about the person you're having the conversation with on a human-to-human level
- **choosing** to be kind over being nice (even if that causes more discomfort)

- **practising** radical candour (from the brilliant work by Kim Scott in her 2017 book *Radical Candor. How to get what you want by saying what you mean*).
- **considering** not just what you say but also how you say it
- **thinking** about the other people that might be impacted too.

Together these four Cs bring us back to a key idea from Chapter 2: great conversations are less about knowing what to do and more about how you show up (*the being part*).

When you bring creativity, courage, challenge and care, the conversation changes, and so does the work.

Part 1 has shown why conversations matter, but also why they often don't happen. As we move into Part 2 and start to think about putting the conversations into practice, it's important to hold onto the fact that **consistency beats perfection, and leadership isn't about one big conversation; it's about all the little ones that come before it.**

Part 2 is about all those *little ones*: the five conversations you need to have, often. And how to have them with confidence.

Part 2

The five key workplace conversations in action

Introduction

In this part of the book, we will take each of the five conversations in turn and bring them to life. But before we do, here are a few things to keep in mind as you go.

Situations

For each conversation, we'll outline some of the most common situations where it might be needed. This won't be an exhaustive list, and you'll come across others too. If you're ever unsure which conversation to have, start it anyway. Don't avoid it. Triage the situation (see page 63 in Chapter 4 for more on this) and see where it takes you both. A step forward is a step closer to where you need to go.

Questions

We will offer some suggested questions – not a script or a comprehensive list, just prompts to help you get started. The next best question is always the one that follows the flow of your conversation. And of course, you can ask them of yourself too.

Tools

We've included three tools for each conversation: the ones we've found useful. They're not the only tools, and they might not be the best fit for your situation. Try them. Adapt them. If you find others that work better, brilliant. Use them... and tell us about them too!

Experiment, adapt, repeat

As you're reading Part 2, remember that it isn't about using everything at once. Some of what we share will be useful. Some might not be right now. Some things will resonate and you'll want to explore further. Others might not yet, and that's OK. Trust your instincts but also keep an open mind. And pay attention to the conversations you're having with yourself, too. They often reveal more than you realise, if you pause and listen.

Happy experimenting...

Chapter 5

Conversations for connection in action

If you only do one thing:

Don't leave connection to chance – make time for it.

In Chapter 4, we talked about how you approach a conversation and how you listen, ask and respond matters just as much as what you say. And that's never truer than when building connection.

Human connection is one of our most basic needs. At work, it's the foundation of trust, belonging and collaboration. These conversations aren't just *nice-to-haves* ;they're critical for engagement, wellbeing and performance.

As Brené Brown puts it in *Daring Greatly* (2015): 'Connection is why we're here; it is what gives purpose and meaning to our lives.'

Whether it's a quick check-in or a longer conversation, the key is to be deliberate. Connection only happens when you make space for it on purpose. This is important in all contexts, but it matters even more in hybrid and remote teams, where those quick catch-ups don't happen by accident. As leaders, we need to be intentional: creating the space for check-ins, not just updates and making sure human-to-human connection isn't lost in the mix of online working and full diaries.

What this conversation is for

Behind every high-performing team is a web of human relationships, and conversations for connection are what strengthen that web. They help you see the human being behind the job title. They build trust and belonging and remind us all that work is something we do with people, not just a lot of tasks.

This isn't about big, emotional moments (though sometimes it might be). It's about what you do consistently. The small, repeated gestures (asking how someone's doing, remembering what matters to them) that build trust and connection and create the strongest foundations, upon which you can build everything else.

Common moments when you'll need it

1. When a new working relationship begins

The aim is: To lay a human foundation before getting into the work (so that when the work happens it's better).

Try asking:

- What's important to you at work?
- What kind of support helps you do your best?
- How do you prefer to give and receive feedback?

2. When someone joins the team or organisation

The aim is: To create a sense of belonging from the start.

Try asking:

- What helps you settle into a new role or team?
- What would make the first three months feel like a success for you?
- What do you need from me to help make that happen?

3. After a change (new role, restructure or personal event)

The aim is: To reconnect and check in on how someone's doing.

Try asking:

- How are things feeling for you right now?
- What support would be most useful at this stage?
- What's helped you in the past that you could draw on now?

4. When someone seems withdrawn, disengaged or out of sorts

The aim is: To open up a discussion.

Try asking:

- What's been going on for you lately?
- I've noticed some changes in X lately – how are things for you?
- What's going well and what would you like to be different at the moment?

5. As part of regular one-to-ones or check-ins

The aim is: To make this type of conversation a habit and build trust through regular, ongoing connection.

Try asking:

- What's something you're proud of right now?
- What's something that's frustrating you at the moment?
- What one thing would make your week/ your role easier or better?

6. When you want to strengthen trust or how the team works together

The aim is: To have this type of conversation at a team level and to encourage team members to connect with each other.

Try asking:

- What's working well for us as a team? What are we proud of?
- What makes this team special/unique?
- What one thing would make our team even stronger?

Questions that make this conversation work

These questions aren't just for big moments, they're ideal for everyday interactions: check-ins, quick chats or when something feels off. They help you get beyond the surface to build real human connection.

- What's important to you at work right now? *(Useful in early one-to-ones or when someone's new to a role.)*
- When do you feel most energised or motivated? *(Great for career development check-ins.)*
- What makes you feel included and supported? *(Great to have as part of team discussions to strengthen belonging and connection.)*

- What kind of feedback is most helpful for you? When receiving feedback, what do you find most useful? *(Good to agree upfront in new relationships or when building trust.)*
- What's something that people often misunderstand about you? *(Great to strengthen relationships and deepen understanding.)*
- What's one thing that would make your week easier or better? *(A great simple, repeatable check-in question for regular conversations.)*
- When do you feel most like yourself at work? *(Great for strengthening relationships and understanding what excites and energises someone.)*

Three tools that might help

These tools can bring more intention and depth to connection conversations. They're simple, human and flexible, and they work.

Tool 1: Personal user manual: how I work at my best

People work, think and communicate differently. But most of the time we either expect others to work in the same way as we do or to know how to work best with us. A personal user manual makes those preferences explicit and visible.

There are lots of tools and assessments that you can use to help open up awareness of your preferences (DISC, Insights and MBTI are some of the most well known) but you can also explore this without any tools. Our favourite way to do this is to use these steps to create a short guide to *you*.

It's a shortcut to helping others understand how you or others work best, and how to provide support, especially in new or changing working relationships.

Putting it into practice:

Complete the prompts below for yourself, then share with a colleague or your team, for example during onboarding, at the start of a project or when working with someone new. You can use it in one-to-ones or in team sessions. Each person fills one out and then you swap and discuss your answers. Then talk about how you might adapt how you work together in practice, using what you've learned.

I do my best work when...

____

____

____

I appreciate it when people...

____

____

____

I find it hard when...

____

____

____

I like feedback to be...

____

____

____

A few things to know about how I work...

____

____

____

A top tip for getting the best out of me is...

____

____

____

Top tip: refer back to it for resetting dynamics if things feel a little off.

Tool 2: Team map: know the humans, not just the roles

You often know what people *do*, but not as much about who they *are*. A team map builds connection by capturing what makes each team member tick: their strengths, motivators and development areas. It helps people appreciate each other as humans, not just job functions, and that's what makes working together easier, more natural and more effective.

Putting it into practice:

Choose three or four of the prompts below (or make up some of your own) to use in team sessions or one-to-ones. Capture key points somewhere visible, for example a shared document or channel, or even a physical wall if you're all together in person.

- What are your strengths or superpowers at work?
- What motivates you the most?
- What do you find drains and recharges your energy the most?
- What is the part of your role that you would always choose over other tasks and why?
- What's one area of your development that you're focusing on this year? And how can others help you with those?
- What does great support look like for you?

Keep it light and voluntary. It's not a personality profile; it's a conversation starter. It's about new insights, not a comprehensive list.

Tool 3: Connection question bank: small questions, big impact

Connection doesn't always come from big, deep and meaningful conversations. Often, it's a small moment that builds trust and shows care. Having a simple set of go-to questions makes it easier to start those moments and to build a habit of using them regularly.

Putting it into practice:

Choose one question to ask at your next one-to-one, meeting or informal chat. Use it at the start or end of the conversation or try it partway through if a meeting is feeling a bit flat.

These questions are just a starting point – so keep adding to them:

- What's been a highlight for you recently?
- What do you need more of, or less of, right now?
- What's something you've been proud of lately?
- What's one thing people might not know about you?
- What gives you energy and what drains it?

Keep these handy and use them often. The more consistent you are, the easier and more natural connection becomes. And over time this helps create a team culture where care and connection are the norm, not just the exception.

Try this: a conversation for connection

Think of someone in your team or network you'd like to reconnect or strengthen connection with. Maybe you're working on something that matters, maybe it feels like there's a bit of friction or maybe you just don't know much about who they are other than their role.

Consider:

What do you already know about what motivates them at work?

____

____

____

What might they need more or less of right now?

____

____

____

What's one simple thing you could do this week to show appreciation or care?

____

____

____

What question from the connection question bank would you like to ask them?

____

____

____

Final thought

In a world increasingly driven by automation, our humanity is our edge, and relationships are what set us apart. Conversations for connection are how we create teams where people feel safe, valued and like they belong – not just as numbers, but as humans.

Chapter 6

Conversations for clarity and alignment in action

If you only do one thing:

Assume you haven't been clear.

Most people think they've communicated clearly. Most actually haven't. Clarity isn't just what you *say*; it's what gets *heard* and then *acted upon*. So, if in doubt, check. No, scrap that... *always* check!

What this conversation is for

This conversation is about making the implicit explicit. It's about checking assumptions, aligning expectations and making sure you're actually working towards the same thing. It happens when work begins, evolves or wobbles. It's not one big *kick-off* conversation; it's a habit of checking in and keeping clear throughout. And in a world of global working and cross-cultural teams that habit matters even more. Time zones, cultural norms and language differences can all amplify a lack of clarity, which makes these conversations essential, not optional.

Common moments when you'll need it

1. At the start of a project or piece of work

The aim is: To get fully aligned on expectations before any work begins.

Try asking:

- What assumptions are we making that haven't been said out loud?
- If we each wrote down the goal we're working towards, would our answers match?
- How will we track progress and share updates?
- What risks could get in the way, and how can we mitigate or tackle them?
- Who else needs to be informed or involved?
- How does this task link to the bigger team or organisational goal?

2. **During a regular catch-up or one-to-one (as part of a project or piece of work)**

The aim is: To stay aligned, to review progress and to adjust where needed.

Try asking:

- What's going well?
- What's not working or feels unclear?
- What's changed since we started?
- What new risks have come up?
- What have we learned so far that we can use?

3. **When you get a sense something is off (at any point during a piece of work)**

The aim is: To realign before things go too far off track.

Try asking:

- What's giving me that gut feel and could there be another explanation?
- How can I check *in* rather than check *on*?
- What would a *curious*, open question look like here?
- What feedback might be helpful, and how can I share it constructively? (*Lots more on this in Chapter 8.*)

4. In a more infrequent appraisal or objective-setting conversation when you get a sense something is off (at any point during a piece of work)

The aim is: To set a clear direction and link short-term goals to the bigger picture.

Try asking:

- What's the outcome we're working towards, and what does success look like?
- How does this goal fit with our team's or organisation's priorities?
- What recent learning should help shape what we do next?
- What feedback themes need to be considered? *(The initial feedback should be in the moment and not stored for appraisals, more on that in Chapter 8.)*

Questions that make this conversation work

These are useful any time you want to check clarity, avoid misalignment or reset expectations. Use them at the start of projects, during check-ins or when things start to drift. They're simple but powerful, especially when used early and often.

- Let's check we have the same understanding. How are you interpreting this? *(Good for spotting misalignment early or for pre-empting it.)*

- What does good look like here? How will you know you have achieved it? *(Great for starting well and agreeing clear expectations upfront.)*
- What are your priorities right now? *(Helps to surface competing demands and where focus might be slipping.)*
- On a scale of 1–10, how confident do you feel about what's expected of you here? What would help increase that number? *(Good for uncovering hidden uncertainty before it becomes an issue.)*
- What do we need to do to make sure we keep on track? *(Great for creating shared accountability and making sure the implicit is explicit.)*
- How will we keep each other updated? *(Good for creating clear, practical ways to stay aligned.)*

Three tools that might help

These tools help you get clear on what matters, who owns what and how the work links to the bigger picture.

Tool 1: Getting clear on priorities

Conversations about priorities are essential because without them, people make their own assumptions about what matters most, or revert to what they enjoy most or feel most comfortable doing. This leads to misalignment, wasted effort and growing frustration.

There are lots of prioritisation tools and frameworks to choose from. The key is to pick one that helps you and your team focus and align on what matters. To get started, use these questions to create more clarity for yourself so you can in turn help others to get clearer.

Putting it into practice:

Think about the following questions for yourself:

What is most important for me/my team to achieve in the next week/month/quarter?

____

____

____

What else is taking up my time or energy that might not really matter?

____

____

____

What's my biggest challenge with prioritising right now? (*It might be saying no, juggling different people's demands, competing priorities.*)

____

____

____

How would I rate myself out of 10 for prioritising well? (1 = poor/10 = great)?

____

What would need to change to move the score up by 1–3 points?

____

____

____

What am I going to do next (one thing I'll start, stop or delegate)?

____

____

____

And once you've done that, share your answers with your team or your line manager and ask:

- Do you agree on what matters most right now?
- What do we need to do to get or stay aligned?

Tool 2: Delegating well

Delegation is one of the clearest ways expectations, ownership and accountability either get clarified or quietly unravel. It's also one of the challenges we're asked about most often: how can I get better at delegation or do it more consistently?

What we find time and again is that the issue usually isn't one of knowledge. Leaders already know what good delegation looks like. What gets in the way is confidence, unhelpful beliefs about letting go of control or about how they can add value if they're not doing the doing – or simply holding on to work they enjoy.

To help you delegate more effectively, here's our seven-step guide to great delegation:

Putting it into practice:

Think about a task you need to delegate: who is best placed to pick this up? Picture them in your mind and work through each step of the seven-step model, capturing notes that might help you when you're having the conversation with your colleague.

____

____

____

What new insights do you have from completing this exercise?

____

____

____

Tool 3: Aligning individual goals with team goals (creating line of sight)

For people to feel engaged, they need to see that what they do matters, by understanding how it connects to something bigger.

That's what *line of sight* means (Boswell et al 2006): making a clear link between an individual's task or goal, the team's success and the organisation's priorities and purpose.

Most of the time this link is left implied. Don't assume people already see the connection. Even if it feels obvious to you, saying it out loud can completely shift how someone sees their work and their value, so make it explicit.

Putting it into practice:

Choose a task, target or goal that one of your team members is working on. Use the prompts below to draw the link from *individual contribution* to *wider impact*.

1. What's the task, goal or responsibility (eg improving customer response times)?

___

___

___

2. How does this help the team to succeed (eg frees up time, supports others, increases capacity)?

___

___

___

3. How does that contribute to the delivery of organisational priorities (eg increases customer satisfaction and loyalty, strengthens brand image, increases customer retention and revenue)?

4. How could you share this link with the individual in a way that feels meaningful and motivating?

Try this: a conversation for clarity and alignment

Pick one project, goal or task you're currently working on with someone in your team. What's the outcome you're both aiming for? What might you not yet have said out loud?

What assumptions might be getting in the way of clarity?

____

____

____

What would you each write down if asked, 'What does good look like here?' Would your answers match?

____

____

____

What's one question you could ask today to check or strengthen alignment?

____

____

____

Final thought

Creating clarity isn't one conversation. It's an ongoing process, a way of leading that assumes things get lost in translation. When you build this into everyday conversations you create alignment that's not just efficient; it allows everyone to do their best work.

Chapter 7

Conversations for development in action

If you only do one thing:

Don't start with the role. Start with the person.

We all have a natural desire to grow – not just to improve performance, but to feel fulfilled, challenged and on a meaningful path. Yet in the workplace, development often gets reduced to technical training plans, annual reviews or vague 'Where do you want to be in five years?' conversations.

Real development conversations go deeper. They start with the person, not the role. It's about helping people reflect, reconnect with their purpose and grow in ways that matter, personally and professionally.

They're energising. They build trust. They unlock potential.

And, as Gabriel Sander, human resources director at global distillery Cuervo, put it in Deloitte's Insights 2024 'When people thrive, business thrives: The case for human sustainability' report: 'Companies can't offer you employment forever, but they should make you employable forever.' (Cantrell et al 2024)

Development conversations are one way to create value for people as human beings, not just as employees. And in a world of continual change, standing still isn't an option for organisations. Technology evolves. Customer expectations increase. New competitors appear. Teams have to keep up, and development conversations create the space for people to experiment, stretch and innovate.

They're most powerful when they're not treated as one-off events. Growth happens through momentum, and the best development conversations often begin as small check-ins, questions or reflections that build over time.

What this conversation is for

Development conversations are about creating space for real growth, not just ticking boxes. They help people:

- make sense of where they are right now in their roles
- spot the gaps they want to close (or need to close to succeed in their role)

- tap into what excites and energises them
- identify their next stretch.

Like the other conversations, these don't need to be long or formal. They work best when time is deliberately set aside, and when they're treated as a regular, human part of how we help people feel seen, supported and stretched.

Common moments when you'll need it

1. As part of regular one-to-ones or career check-ins

The aim is: To create space for reflection, exploration and growth.

Try asking:

- What part of your work feels most meaningful right now?
- What do you want to be known for?
- What would growth look like for you over the next few months?

2. During or after performance reviews

The aim is: To shift from *what happened* or *what was* to *what's next.*

Try asking:

- Which part of that feedback feels most important to focus on?

- Which part of the feedback landed most for you?
- What do you want to be different next time?

3. When someone feels stuck, bored or underused

The aim is: To reignite motivation and uncover what gives someone energy.

Try asking:

- What energises you? What drains you?
- Think back to a time when you felt in the zone. What made it feel that way?
- What kind of experience would stretch you?

4. After a promotion, role change or stretch project

The aim is: To support an individual to gain confidence.

Try asking:

- What would success in this role/project look like for you?
- What do you want to be saying in six months/at the end of the project?
- What support would help?

5. When someone expresses interest in growth or learning

The aim is: To explore possibilities and turn interest into action.

Try asking:

- What are you curious to learn more about?
- What ideas do you have for how we could improve?
- What would make this next step feel exciting rather than overwhelming?

6. When you notice untapped potential

The aim is: To invite growth without pressure.

Try asking:

- What do you think might be holding you back from X?
- If you were being brave, what might you do next?
- I've noticed X. Is that something you'd like to develop further?

Questions that make this conversation work

Use these anytime you want to help someone create insight, build excitement or think about what's next. Use them in career conversations, project check-ins and reviews or whenever it feels time to support someone to explore what's next.

- What have you learned about yourself recently? *(Good for reflecting on what recent work or stretch has revealed.)*
- Where do you feel underused right now, and where do you feel stretched? *(Helps surface current fit and potential growth areas.)*
- What feels like it's starting to matter more to you now than it did before? *(Good for surfacing shifting priorities and motivation.)*
- Where are you feeling ready for more stretch right now? *(Helps you see where they're ready to grow next.)*
- What skills or experiences would you be excited to build next? *(Helps identify development that feels motivating, not imposed.)*
- How do your current goals line up with what matters to you outside of work? *(Supports sustainable, values-led development.)*
- What do you need from me to help you take the next step? *(Helps turn insight into action and shared responsibility.)*

Tip: Listen for what lights them up. Development isn't just about skills; it's about values, identity and motivation.

Three tools that might help

These tools add a light structure to development conversations, creating space for reflection and clearer choices about what to focus on next.

Tool 1: Surfacing the development gap using the Johari window

Self-awareness is at the heart of growth, and the Johari window (developed by psychologists Joseph Luft and Harry Ingham in 1955) is a simple tool that helps people explore what they know about themselves, what others see and what might still be hidden.

It's a brilliant way to open up development conversations, giving structure, creating space for feedback and reflection, and helping people spot growth areas that might otherwise stay under the surface. And in doing so it builds a clearer, shared picture of where to go next.

It's made up of four parts, or *quadrants*:

- **Open:** What I know about myself, and others do too.
- **Blind spot:** What others see, but I don't.
- **Hidden:** What I know, but choose not to share.
- **Unknown:** What's not yet known to me or others *(often where untapped potential or hidden strengths sit)*.

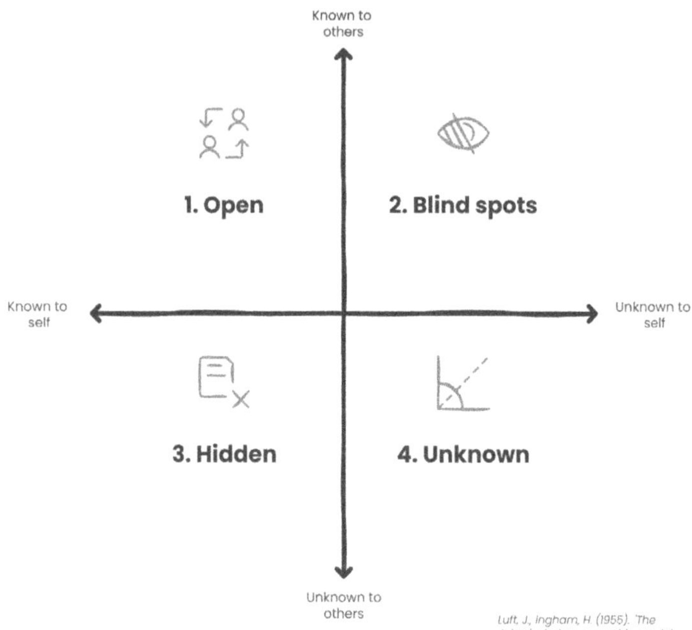

Luft, J., Ingham, H. (1955). 'The Johari window, a graphic model of interpersonal awareness'.

The aim is to grow the *open* area by sharing more, being open to feedback and exploring what might still be *unknown*.

Putting it into practice:

You can use the Johari window in two ways:

- with a team member to explore blind spots, hidden strengths and areas for growth. Start by explaining the essence of the model and then explore each quadrant together, using these prompts to guide the conversation.

➤ for yourself by reflecting on the same questions to uncover insights about your own strengths and areas for growth.

1. **Open** (what I know about myself, and others do too)

These are the strengths, behaviours and ways of working that feel familiar and visible.

Try asking a colleague or reflecting for yourself on:

- What do you know you're good at and that others regularly see in you?
- What feedback have you received recently that confirmed something you already knew?
- What part of your role, kind of work or situations bring out your best?

If you were exploring your own development, what might be your responses to the questions above?

____

____

____

2. **Blind spots** (what others see but I don't)

These are things that others might see, or behaviours that they might experience but you might not be aware of yet.

Try asking a colleague or reflecting for yourself on:

- What feedback have you received recently, and what surprised you?
- What do people often come to you for advice or help with?
- What's a strength that others see in you that you sometimes overlook?
- Is there feedback you've heard more than once that you've found hard to accept or believe?

If you were exploring your own development, what might be your responses to the questions above?

____

____

____

3. Hidden (what I know but choose not to share)

These are the things you know about yourself but haven't shared openly at work... yet.

Try asking a colleague or reflecting for yourself on:

- What's something you're good at but rarely get to use in your role?
- What do you wish people at work understood about you?
- What kind of work do you secretly enjoy or miss?

- Is there anything holding you back that others might not be aware of?

If you were exploring your own development, what might be your responses to the questions above?

____

____

____

4. **Unknown** (what's not yet known to me or others)

This is where untapped potential might still be hiding.

Try asking a colleague or reflecting for yourself on:

- What kind of challenge would stretch you right now?
- What haven't you tried yet that you'd like to?
- When was the last time you surprised yourself? What happened?
- What new experience could unlock something new for you?

If you were exploring your own development, what might be your responses to the questions above?

____

____

____

What new insights do you have from exploring the four quadrants of the Johari window?

____

____

____

What is the first action you want to take as a result?

____

____

____

Tool 2: A personal SWOT

The SWOT analysis (developed by Albert Humphrey in the 1960s) is a well-known tool, but one that is often underused in development conversations. It offers another way to open up conversations and bring structure to support personal reflection and explore self-awareness and aspirations, alongside potential gaps and risks.

Originally developed as a strategic planning tool to assess the internal and external factors affecting a business or project, a SWOT (Strengths, Weaknesses, Opportunities, Threats) can be just as impactful for an individual.

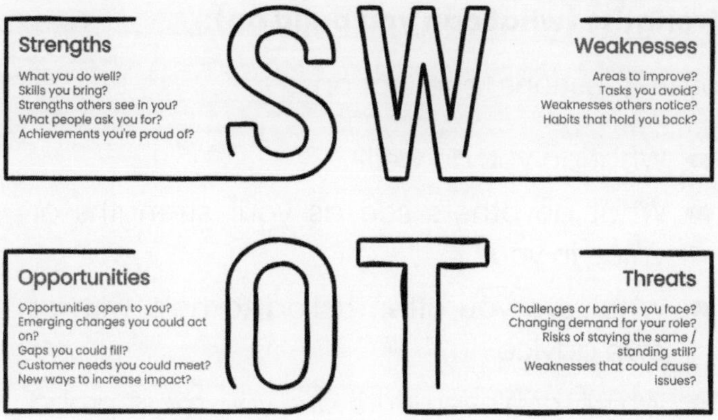

Putting it into practice:

If the Johari window is great for increasing self-awareness and creating opportunities for feedback, then the SWOT is useful for when someone is a bit stuck, wants to stretch themselves and wants to think about what to focus on next.

Both bring a gentle structure, but SWOT is the one to go for when you want to support someone (or yourself) to take stock of what's working and where the biggest possibilities are. And again, it works well as a guided development conversation exercise or a self-reflection tool that you both discuss afterwards.

When using it to support a colleague, start by explaining the framework and discussing how it can be adapted to focus on an individual's development and then explore each element. It works just as well as a self-reflection exercise.

Strengths (what can you build on):

Some questions to reflect on:

- What do you do well?
- What do others see as your strengths or value in you?
- What are you often asked to help with or give advice on?
- Which achievements are you most proud of, and what helped you achieve them?

Capture the reflections and insights about strengths that emerge:

____

____

____

Weaknesses (what might hold you back):

Some questions to reflect on:

- What do you know you could improve on?
- What do you find difficult or avoid when you can?
- What have you been given feedback on more than once?
- What habits or behaviours could get in your way if left unchecked?

Capture the reflections and insights about weaknesses that emerge:

____

____

____

Opportunities (what could you stretch into):

Some questions to reflect on:

- What new experiences or opportunities are available to you right now?
- What emerging trends could create new possibilities?
- How could you make more of your current network or grow it further?
- What needs or gaps in your team, company or industry could you help fill?
- What different ways of working could increase your impact?

Capture the reflections and insights about opportunities that emerge:

____

____

____

Threats (what could get in your way):

Some questions to reflect on:

- What current challenges or risks could get in the way or slow your progress?
- Is the demand for what you do or your role changing?
- What might happen if nothing changes? How might you be left behind?
- Are any of your current *weaknesses* creating a risk?

Capture the reflections and insights about threats that emerge:

____

____

____

Looking across all four areas, explore their biggest insights or surprises.

____

____

____

What is the first action they want to take as a result?

____

____

____

Tool 3: Fast, reflective check-ins

As we have explored throughout this book, great conversations don't have to be big moments. One simple way to bring more focus to development is to regularly include three quick-fire questions in your one-to-ones or team meetings.

Here are some options you can choose from, or adapt to create your own version:

Past – present – future

Good for tracking progress and encouraging deeper reflection.

- **Past:** What's something you've felt proud of this week or month? What's been a moment of growth for you recently?
- **Present:** When or where are you at your best right now? Where are you feeling a bit stuck or unsure?
- **Future:** What would you love a bit more of in your day to day? Where could you stretch yourself over the next few weeks or months?

High – low – learn

Good for helping people talk more openly about the highs and lows.

- **High:** What's been a high point for you recently?
- **Low:** What's been tough or felt like a bit of a low point?

- **Learn:** What did you take from both of those experiences? Anything you'd do differently next time?

Radiator – drain – rebalance

Good for supporting wellbeing or during periods of high demand or change.

- **Radiator:** What's been giving you energy recently?
- **Drain:** What's been draining your energy or has left you feeling flat?
- **Rebalance:** What's one thing you've learned about how to create more balance or protect your energy?

Tried – learned – stuck

Good for stretching confidence and supporting the learning gained from new experiences.

- **Tried:** What's something new you've had a go at recently?
- **Learned:** What's one thing you've learned about yourself through that?
- **Stuck:** What still feels tricky or uncertain that you'd like to figure out?

Start – stop – continue

Good for prioritising, planning or making progress on goals.

- **Start:** What's something new you want to try out?

- **Stop:** What's no longer working or not helping that you could stop?
- **Continue:** What's working well that you want to keep doing more of?

Highlight – hurdle – habit

Good for building positive routines and reinforcing progress.

- **Highlight:** What's been the highlight of your week or month?
- **Hurdle:** What's got in your way, or what challenge have you overcome?
- **Habit:** What's one new habit or tweak that could make next month even better?

Try this: a conversation for development

1. For someone in your team

Think of someone in your team who you want to support to grow. It might be in confidence or capability, or it might be about helping them to think about what they do next. Reflect on:

What is most important to them right now, both inside and outside of work? And how do you know? (Have you asked them or are you making an assumption?) How might you find out more?

____

____

____

What sort of challenge, opportunity or stretch might help them?

____

____

____

What's one question you could ask to help them reflect on their own development?

____

____

____

What is something that they've done recently that shows progress or potential? How could you share this with them?

____

____

____

2. For yourself

Think about something you have done recently that you're proud of or that felt like you stretched yourself. What insights does it offer about your strengths, preferences or the progress you have made?

What part of your work feels most meaningful to you right now?

Where do you feel energised right now, and where do you feel you've more to give?

What does growth look like for you over the next three to six months? And what experience, challenge or support would you need to help you achieve this?

What's the first step you could take (or the first conversation you need to have) as a result of this reflection?

Final thought

Great development conversations don't have to be long or complicated, but they do need to be human. They're not about ticking boxes or talking in vague hypotheticals. They're about creating space for people to reflect, dream, stretch and grow in ways that genuinely matter.

Done well, these conversations don't just shape careers; they reconnect people to what matters: right now, and for what comes next.

Chapter 8

Conversations for performance improvement in action

If you only do one thing:

Remember: you get what you tolerate.

There's no getting away from it – performance improvement conversations are often the hardest ones to have. They're the ones that cause the most anxiety, that many leaders feel the least equipped for, carry the most weight and the highest perceived risk.

'What if it goes wrong? What if I say the wrong thing? What if I make things worse?'

But (and it's a big but), you won't improve things if you don't have the conversation. The things you might fear will happen if you do have it (emotions escalating, loss of trust, team morale dips, relationship damage) are all things that will almost certainly happen if you don't. And the conversation you need to have never gets easier on its own. Time and avoidance just make it harder later. As the saying goes, and as Susan Scott highlights in *Fierce Conversations* (2017), what you're willing to tolerate is what you get.

And layered on top of that is the fact that teams are more multigenerational than ever, bringing different expectations and experiences of work. Therefore, approaching performance improvement conversations requires adaptability: meeting people where they are, leading with kindness and keeping the focus on the what, not the who. Let's explore how to do that...

What this conversation is for

- to help someone understand how they're doing in their role
- to explore what sits behind a gap in performance, not just point it out
- to support someone to step up, not feel small
- to help someone see where they shine.

These conversations are often misunderstood as being all about telling someone where they got it wrong or fell short. But they're not just about what you have to say; they're about what happens between you *and* your colleague in the conversation. They're about choosing to be kind rather than just *nice* and they're about prioritising honesty over harmony. When done well, these conversations aren't about blame; they're about openness and collaboration. It's not 'You messed up'; it's 'Let's look at this together'. And it's not about *them* as a person; it's about the *thing that happened*.

Remember and hold on to this: you're not aiming for agreement; you're aiming for **acknowledgement**. The other person doesn't need to see it exactly as you do. What matters is that they can see enough to recognise that there is a gap and that something needs to change (see Chapter 4's discussion around the *gap* – page 69). That's when you can move forward.

These conversations aren't only about identifying what needs to improve. They're just as much about naming what's working and highlighting the value people bring, especially when they might not see it for themselves. And as in other chapters, these don't have to be big moments… in fact, the longer you leave them, the bigger they get.

Common moments when you'll need it

1. **When there is a gap between what's required and what's happening in practice** *(whether it's because expectations have changed or something else is getting in the way)*

The aim is: To name the gap and work out together what needs to change, and how to make that change happen.

Try asking:

- Can I share something I've noticed?
- What's your perspective on that?
- Which part would you like my support with?

2. **When there is a dip in performance and you don't know why**

The aim is: To find out what's really going on, without assuming anything.

Try asking:

- What's it like in your world right now?
- What's going on that I might not be seeing?
- What do you need from me right now?

3. **When you start to notice a pattern and want to *catch it* before it becomes a bigger issue**

The aim is: To spot the early signs and talk about it before it escalates.

Try asking:

- I've noticed something a couple of times now; can we talk it through?
- What's your take on what's happening?
- What's going to help get things back on track?

4. When others are being affected by someone's behaviour

The aim is: To raise awareness of impact, open up potential blind spots and think together about what to do differently.

Try asking:

- Can I share the impact I think this is having?
- What's it like from your perspective?
- What could you do differently next time?

5. When you want to highlight something positive that someone isn't recognising

The aim is: To help someone see and value the impact they're having.

Try asking:

- I appreciated (*what you observed*). Can I tell you why?
- What do you take from that?
- Where else could that have an impact? How else could you use it?

6. **When someone is doing well and you want to stretch or challenge them further**

The aim is: To share belief in someone, build confidence and support their next step.

Try asking:

- What would feel like a good stretch for you right now?
- How could you have even more impact?
- What would you like to be saying about your development in six months' time?

Questions that make this conversation work

A list of questions here would be at odds with how we see this conversation. For us, it starts with honesty and clarity: put the thing you want to talk about on the table, get clear together on the *gap* (see Chapter 4, page 69), then on what needs to change next. It's more about how you show up than the exact words you use. These conversations aren't about catching someone out or showing *who's in charge*. They're about opening up a discussion so you can move towards what matters most: what you both do next.

So, rather than a list of questions in isolation, go straight to the tools below, especially Tool 3: The CAIRD model, which suggests questions in the context of the whole conversation. Or, if you're unsure whether to have the conversation in the first place, start instead with Tool 1: Pre-conversation checklist.

Three tools that might help

These tools help you decide when a performance improvement conversation is needed, and support you to approach it with clarity, care and intent.

Tool 1: Making sure a performance improvement conversation is the right approach (using a pre-conversation checklist)

Sometimes we avoid a performance conversation because it feels uncomfortable, and sometimes we avoid it because, deep down, we're not sure it's the *right* thing to do. This quick checklist helps you tell the difference: distinguishing between *discomfort* (which will never fully go away) and genuine *doubt* about whether this is the right conversation at the right time and in the right way.

Think of it as part of the triage process we talked about in Chapter 4 (page 63). It's not about overthinking or second-guessing yourself; it's a quick sense check, a structured way to pause, reflect and ask yourself: 'Am I approaching this in the right way, for the right reasons and with the information I need to make it as useful as possible for the person receiving it?'

If you're feeling hesitant, it doesn't mean the conversation shouldn't happen. It might just mean it needs to happen with more clarity, more care or more preparation.

Pre-conversation checklist:

Ask yourself:

1. How might I feel receiving this (is it fair, is it honest, is the timing right, is it the right message, is it valid)?
2. Is my intention positive?
3. Am I making assumptions about this person and their abilities, decisions or behaviours that might be inaccurate?
4. Have I set realistic goals?
5. Have I made my expectations clear?
6. How can I share this in a way that focuses on the situation and not the person?
7. Am I being specific about what I am seeing or noticing, or am I making broad generalisations?
8. Is this feedback useful?
9. Is this actually a conduct/compliance issue that needs a more formal HR process? If the answer to this one is yes or you're not sure, then follow policy and seek advice.

Putting it into practice:

Next time you need to raise a performance concern, take a few minutes to look through this checklist. If it raises any questions, take a moment and adjust your message. It's not about softening what you say; it's about making sure you're having the *right* conversation in the *right* way.

Tool 2: Opening up different perspectives using the different chairs technique

Sometimes the hardest part of a performance improvement conversation isn't describing what's happening (or not happening); it's helping someone actually see it, and the impact it's having, from a perspective other than their own.

The different chairs technique (rooted in Gestalt work and referenced by Pugh 2017) is a simple way to shift perspective. It does this by inviting someone to consider the view from someone else's *seat*, whether that's a client or customer, a teammate, another colleague or even you.

And it helps with one of the biggest barriers to improving performance, when a person isn't denying what's happening but they just can't see why it matters. This is where you need to hold on to what we mentioned earlier in this chapter: you're aiming for **acknowledgement**, not agreement. This isn't about getting them to agree with your point of view; it's about opening up the space to explore how things might look or feel from a different angle.

It's particularly useful when someone can't see why something needs to change because they're unaware of the impact it's having.

Let's think about an example:

Situation: Someone in your team regularly interrupts others in meetings. It's frustrating colleagues and stifling discussion.

You raise it and they say: 'I'm just really enthusiastic and full of ideas. I don't see what's wrong with that. If others have something to say, they just need to say it.'

In that moment, they can't see past their own view, and pushing harder to convince them won't help.

So instead, try a different chair:

You might say: 'I get that, and we absolutely want your ideas. We also want to make space for others to share theirs too. Let's imagine we're sitting in your colleague's seat, the one who was cut off a few times in the meeting this morning. How might it have felt for them?'

Even better, if it feels appropriate, invite them to physically move to another chair.

'Let's imagine this chair here is your colleague's. Can you sit in it for a moment? From there, how might that experience have felt for them?'

Then pause and see what opens up.

Putting it into practice:

Think about a situation you're dealing with right now that feels frustrating, difficult or a bit off. Who else is impacted by this situation?

____

____

____

Move to a different chair that represents their position. What might the situation look like for them from here?

____

____

____

What new insights does that give you?

____

____

____

What's the first step you want to take as a result?

____

____

____

Next time you, or someone in your team, seems stuck in their own viewpoint, try inviting them into a different chair. Choose a perspective that matters, someone who might be impacted. You're not forcing them to see what you see; you're just helping them widen their view.

Tool 3: Getting clear on the message you want to share using the CAIRD model

When it comes to performance improvement conversations, it's not just what you say, it's the conversation it opens up and what happens next that matters. Any framework for structuring feedback needs to be a guide, not a script. It should help you shape a clear message without making it rigid or robotic. And so, the simpler, the better.

You might have come across some well-known models:

- AID (Landsberg 1996): Action, Impact, Desired Outcome.
- SBI (The Center for Creative Leadership): Situation, Behaviour, Impact.
- CEDAR (Woodruffe 2006): Context, Examples, Diagnosis, Action, Review.

All have value. For us though, the missing piece is that they can focus too much on delivering the message. We want a two-way conversation. That's why we've combined the best parts into a version that is clear *and* conversational: the CAIRD model.

The CAIRD model: Context, Action, Impact, Response, Do differently

- **Context:** Set the stage. Why this conversation and why now?
- **Action:** What have you seen or noticed? Be specific.

- **Impact:** What effect is it having – on others, the work or you? Again, be concrete and clear. This is often the trickiest part to say, and the most important for helping the gap land so you can move on to what comes next.
- **Response:** Invite their perspective. What's their take on it?
- **Do differently:** Be clear about what needs to change. (See page 147 for more on when and how to use this part of the model and what to do if the conversation gets stuck.)

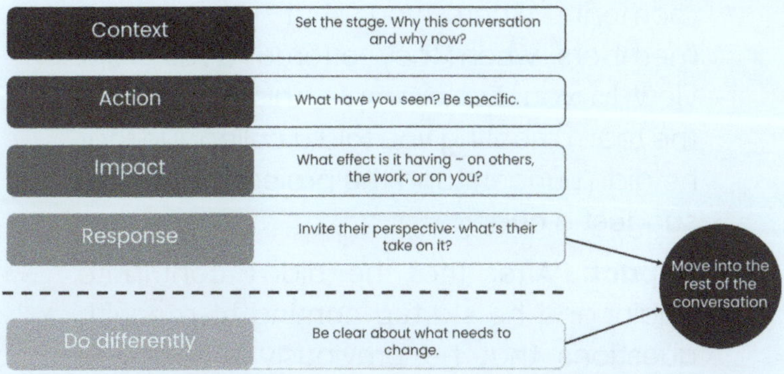

We use the CAIRD model to deliver a clear message *and then* open up a two-way discussion, not to assume you have all the answers. It puts the topic on the table so you can stand side by side together and move it forward.

Let's think about what this might look like in an example:

Scenario: A strong performer in your team has a very direct style when they disagree in meetings.

You've noticed they sometimes cut across junior colleagues and as a result those colleagues are contributing less and are now bringing questions and issues to you instead. This is increasing your workload into areas outside of your remit and priorities.

- **Context:** 'I value the contributions you make to the team and I am keen to support you to have as much impact as possible so I'd like to share an observation.'
- **Action:** 'In the last week I noticed two moments where you shut down team members when they offered a different view to you. For example, this morning in the team meeting you told a colleague that he didn't understand the project enough to suggest a change.'
- **Impact:** 'After that, he didn't contribute again, and he started coming to me with questions that he previously brought to you. That reduces his input and adds to my workload.'
- **Response:** 'What's your perspective? What's going on for you in that moment?'
- **Do differently:** 'To make sure everyone in the team feels safe to contribute ideas, I need you to consider other perspectives rather than closing them down. Shall we spend some time thinking about how you might do that?'

Putting it into practice:

Think of a conversation you need to have, one that you have been putting off – maybe because it feels uncomfortable or awkward, or you don't know how to start.

Now use the CAIRD model as a way to get crystal clear on the message you want to share. Go through each of the five elements and write it out as if you were talking directly to the person.

This isn't a script to read from; it's a way to sort your thoughts, get intentional with the language you want to use and refine the message so you don't over-soften or dilute it.

Write a couple of sentences under each heading:

Context: Set the stage. Why now? What's prompted the conversation?

____

____

____

Action: What specifically have you seen, heard or noticed?

____

____

____

Impact: Why does it matter, what effect is it having – on others, the work or you?

____

____

____

Response: How will you invite their perspective?

____

____

____

Do differently: What needs to happen next or what needs to change?

____

____

____

Read it aloud. Does it sound honest, clear and natural? Tweak it until it does. Maybe even share it with someone else to get their perspective on how it might be received.

The aim isn't to memorise it; it's preparation so you can be confident in what you want to say, and can start calm and able to focus on what happens *in* the conversation, not just what you say at the start.

What if that doesn't work?

Now you have an example of a performance improvement conversation and a way of preparing and practising. But when we were in leadership roles, feedback models always seemed to feel a bit *lacking* in some way, and the work we have done since has allowed us to understand why.

A model suggests that if we follow it we will succeed; however, conversations for performance improvement don't always go to plan, and that's not because anyone did anything wrong. Even with the best preparation and the clearest message, people don't always respond the way we hope.

That's why the *'Try this'* in this chapter is a little different from the previous chapters.

Instead of helping you plan a conversation, this one helps you prepare for how to respond, depending on where the conversation goes, and what to do if it gets stuck.

Try this: what to do when a conversation for performance improvement gets stuck

The CAIRD model helps you stay clear and constructive, but people aren't predictable. They're human, and they're driven by emotion. We love this quote by Heen & Stone from their 2014 *Harvard Business Review* article 'Finding the Coaching in the Criticism' because it explains why this happens so well:

> 'Feedback is challenging because it sits at the crossroads of two human needs: 1. the need to learn and grow and 2. the need to be accepted just as we are.'

Receiving feedback hits right at that crossroads, and as a result, we often see (and have experienced ourselves) one of three things happening when you get to the R (Response) stage of the CAIRD model.

Here's what we mean, and what to do next:

What happens at *Response*	**What it sounds / looks like**	**What to do**
1. Your colleague gets it straight away.	The gap is acknowledged and you can then both move forward.	You may not need to use the D (Do differently) in full. Move naturally to what happens next.
2. Your colleague doesn't see the feedback exactly as you do but there is acknowledgement.	There's some defensiveness or resistance initially, but ultimately acceptance that something needs to change.	Move to D calmly. Be clear about what needs to change and then together agree the next step.
3. Your colleague doesn't accept the feedback, and the conversation gets stuck.	Pushback, shut down or denial. No acknowledgement of the gap or need for change.	After stating D clearly, suggest a pause to let emotions settle. Revisit the conversation (ideally within 24 hours).

We've seen (and experienced) so many conversations go off track at point 3. The instinct is to push harder, to try and convince, while your colleague becomes quieter and more resistant and the conversation gets more stuck.

Instead, try pausing. Not to avoid the issue, but to create space for reflection, perspective and for some of the immediate emotions to settle. In practice this might look like:

'This is a tough, but important conversation. Let's both take an hour and come back to it this afternoon.'

Or: 'Why don't we pause for today so we can both let this settle. I want us both to have a bit of space to think about what we want to happen next, so let's pick it up tomorrow.'

The person you're having the conversation with may not magically change their view, but the pause takes the heat out of the moment and gives you both a better chance of moving forward together.

Final thought

If you wait to make these conversations perfect before you start them, the reality is you'll probably never have them. They will *always* feel uncomfortable, because you care and you're human. So channel that care into how you approach them.

Performance conversations aren't about making someone feel bad. They're about standing side by side and looking at something together. It's not about being nice; it's about being clear and kind. And kind is caring enough to give someone the chance to improve.

Chapter 9

Conversations for problem solving in action

If you only do one thing:

Remember: if you keep doing the work, then they're not learning how to.

We talked about this a lot in Chapter 4, especially when we introduced the idea of the *hot potato* (on page 71). The reality is that sometimes (or most of the time) we're the source of the frustrations we're feeling. We often hear leaders say, 'I need my team to take more ownership.' But more often than not, it's the way they're leading that gets in the way of their team from actually taking it.

It's an easy trap to fall into. Someone brings you a problem, and because you want to be helpful, or you're short on time, you give them the answer. And just like that, you're now holding the problem. But when you're holding it, they're not... and they're not learning how to either. When we jump in to fix or solve, we're taking ownership, whether we realise it or not.

In a world where AI gives us more data and options that ever before, we need to remember: technology can provide the insights and the choices but it can't replace the human side of problem solving. It's the conversations we have that make sense of those insights and turn them into actions that work in our unique contexts.

And just to be clear: what we're calling *problem-solving conversations* might also be labelled *coaching conversations*.

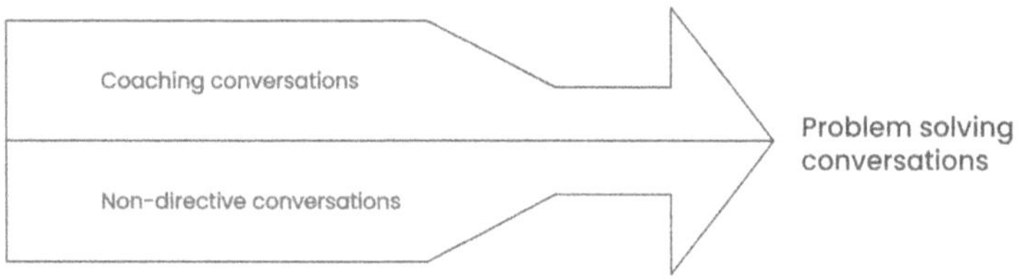

What this conversation is for

Problem-solving conversations are about handing back the *hot potato*. They help people think for themselves, take ownership and develop in the process. That absolutely doesn't mean leaving them to flounder or fail. It means supporting them to step up, not back.

These conversations don't need to be formal or long. As with many of the other conversations, it's the small, in-the-moment questions that create the biggest shifts. It might be that the way you bring it into your day-to-day is to lead with a question and then see what that opens up, for example:

'Here's what you need to do'

becomes

'What have you thought of already?'

It's about making space for thinking, not rushing to a solution. It requires us to shift our mindset from 'It's my job to have the answer' to 'They have the potential to solve this'. When this becomes part of how you lead, it's one of the few ways to reclaim the most limited leadership resource: time.

Common moments when you'll need it

Problem-solving conversations are often reactive, as the opportunity can appear in the moment. When it does, the key is to pause so you can catch up with yourself, rather than defaulting to telling or fixing.

1. When your instinct is to jump in and rescue or fix

The aim is: To create space to think, instead of taking over.

Try asking:

- What's the question you're trying to answer here?
- Which part of this is the trickiest?

- What support would be most useful from me right now?

2. **When someone comes to you with a problem they can't solve**

The aim is: To help them build confidence and take ownership.

Try asking:

- What have you already considered or tried?
- What does good look like here?
- What is the first step you could take?

3. **When someone feels stuck or overwhelmed by a decision**

The aim is: To help them to break it down into something more manageable so they can take action.

Try asking:

- Which part of this feels most difficult?
- What have you dealt with before that is like this?
- What options have you thought about so far?

4. When the same issue or question keeps coming back to you

The aim is: To break the pattern and move responsibility to where it needs to sit.

Try asking:

- What's stopping you from resolving this?
- What do you think would help stop this coming back?
- What's your part in making this happen?

5. When people are escalating things too quickly

The aim is: To encourage self or peer problem solving and reduce dependency on you.

Try asking:

- Who else could help you work this through?
- Where should this conversation really be happening and with whom?
- What would you do if I wasn't available?

6. When you want to help others feel part of something or when the responsibility needs to sit with someone else

The aim is: To build shared ownership.

Try asking:

- What would good look like for you?
- And what would be the impact of achieving that?
- What could get in the way and how could you work around it?

7. **When there is an opportunity to help someone grow, not just get something done**

The aim is: To stretch and develop capability and confidence.

Try asking:

- What learning do you want to take away from this?
- Which part of this might stretch you?
- What help do you need?

When you won't need it

This style of conversation, more exploratory and less directive, can be used far more often than we realise. So, it might be more helpful to flip the question to: when is it *not* the right approach?

In our view, there are three of these moments:

1. When there is a crisis or time-critical situation

In a genuine emergency, time and risk are the priority. Clarity matters most, and giving direction is not only appropriate, it's necessary.

2. When the individual genuinely lacks the knowledge, skills or experience to find a solution

This isn't about whether they've done this exact thing before. It's about whether they have *anything* to draw on: from previous roles, projects or even life outside of work. Before you default to fixing, ask yourself, 'What assumptions am I making? Could I be underestimating what they could be capable of?' Remember *triaging* from Chapter 4 (page 63). It comes in useful here.

3. When there is only one way to do something

Sometimes compliance, safety or technical constraints leave no room for interpretation. But again, it's important to pause and check your assumptions. Is there really only one way or just the only way you know of right now?

If, hand on heart, you know this moment calls for clarity and direction, then be directive. That's part of the conversation spectrum too (we just focus less on it here because it's where we're instinctively drawn). But that doesn't mean the opportunity for a problem-solving conversation is lost. You can still come back to it later, even briefly, to:

- reflect together on what happened and what learning there is to take
- explore how they approached it and what they might do differently next time.
- help them build confidence for future situations.

These small follow-up moments matter. They reinforce that learning is ongoing, that conversations are always worth having and that their growth matters, even when time is tight.

Questions that make this conversation work

There are plenty of frameworks to help structure non-directive conversations. The best known is probably GROW (Whitmore 1992) but others include CLEAR (Hawkins 2011) and OSCAR (Gilbert & Whittleworth 2002).

We've taken the best bits of those and created our own: the **CAPE conversation approach**.

Why another one? While the others work brilliantly in more *formal* coach–client relationships, we've found from experience that they don't always fit the informal, fast-paced reality of workplace conversations, especially when you're trying to help someone think through a tricky issue without jumping in to fix.

This is where the CAPE conversation approach comes in. It gives just enough structure to guide a helpful non-directive conversation without feeling too rigid.

C **CLARIFY** context and area under discussion

A **ACTIVATE** awareness

P **PROBE**

E **EMPOWER** to take forward

Rather than treating this as a script, think of the CAPE conversation approach as a lens. The questions below give you options to draw from across the four elements, depending on what the moment calls for:

C - Clarify the context and area under discussion:
Start by slowing things down and helping them get clear on what's really going on.
Try asking:
- What's the question you're trying to answer?
- What would you like to be different?
- What does success look like?
- What feels at stake for you in this?
- So, what's the real issue here for you?
- What would be most useful from me right now?

A - Activate awareness:
Help them step back and see the situation more clearly
Try asking:
- What's the impact this is having, on you or others?
- What's making this feel tricky or stuck?
- What have you already tried?
- What's in your control, and what isn't?
- Have you faced anything like this before? What helped then?
- Which of your strengths could help you here?

P – Probe to go deeper:
Encourage them to look at things from a new angle and to dig deeper.
Try asking:
- What options are there, even imperfect ones?
- What would you do if you weren't worried about getting it wrong?
- What's the risk of doing nothing?
- What's really getting in the way?
- What's just outside your comfort zone here?
- If someone else brought this to you, what would you suggest?

E – Empower to take forward:
End the conversation with clarity, commitment, and confidence.
Try asking:
- What's the first step you will take, and by when?
- What might get in the way, and how could you work around it?
- What support do you need?
- How will you make sure that happens?
- What will help you stay on track with this?
- What's been most useful from this conversation?

Three tools that might help

These tools help you slow down the urge to fix, widen the thinking and support problem-solving while keeping ownership where it belongs.

Tool 1: Bringing in different perspectives using the Six Thinking Hats technique

One of the biggest barriers to problem solving is getting stuck in narrow thinking. Often, the ideas we need are just outside our current frame of reference. In workshops, we often use the image of a racehorse with its blinkers on, focused on their immediate task but unable to see what's outside of its immediate line of sight. Once we've stepped back from the urge to jump in and fix, one of the most helpful things we can do is help the other person *lift the blinkers,* to consider different angles, perspectives or positions before jumping to a conclusion. In doing so, we bring in more than just our (often limited) assumptions or viewpoints in that moment of stuckness.

This is where the Six Thinking Hats technique comes in.

Originally developed by Edward de Bono, this simple framework gives us a structure, and the prompts, to explore a problem from six different angles. You use it by metaphorically switching *hats*, and with each one, shifting your thinking to match it. The aim is to make sure nothing important is missed or overlooked.

Here's a simplified version of what each hat stands for:

Hat	What it represents	Questions that help to explore it
White	Facts and information	What do we know? What do we need to find out?
Yellow	Optimism, positives and benefits	What are the benefits? What opportunities are there?
Black	Risks, difficulties and problems	What could go wrong? What are the risks?
Red	Feelings, emotions and intuition	How do I feel about this? What is my gut telling me?
Green	Creativity, ideas and alternatives	What else could we try? How could we approach it differently?
Blue	The overview, the thinking process	Where are we in our thinking? What needs to happen next?

And, of course, you don't have to use all six hats every time. Sometimes it only takes you to switch hats once or twice to shift your thinking, bring in a new perspective and get unstuck.

Putting it into practice:

As with many of the tools in this book, you can use this one to think through a problem yourself or to support someone else to.

Try it for yourself.

Choose a challenge or problem that feels unclear or sticky.

Work through each of the Six Thinking Hats one at a time. For some you might pause briefly. For others you may want to go deeper. The goal isn't to spend equal time on each; it's to make sure nothing that could be useful gets overlooked.

White hat (facts and information)

- What do I know (with evidence to back it up rather than assumptions I am making)?
- What do I need to find out?

____

____

____

Yellow hat (optimism, positives and benefits)

- What are the benefits, rewards or upsides?
- What would be the impact of this being a success?

____

____

____

Black hat (risks, difficulties and problems)

- What could go wrong?
- What risks might I not be seeing?

____

____

____

Red hat (feelings, emotions and instinct)

- What's my gut telling me?
- How is this making me feel (and how might that be impacting my choices)?

____

____

____

Green hat (creativity, ideas and alternatives)

- What else could I try?
- If I was being brave, what would I do?

____

____

____

Blue hat (the thinking process itself)

- What's shifted in my thinking?
- What needs to happen next?

____

____

____

Here is some space to capture any reflections and/or insights about the exercise:

____

____

____

Supporting someone else with their thinking

You don't have to explain the full framework (though you can). And you don't need to use all six hats. Think of it more as a tool to gently shift the conversation whenever it feels stuck.

Here are a few ways to experiment and find what works for you.

- In one-to-ones or check-ins try using some of the question prompts above to bring in a new perspective. For example:

'Let's both wear the green hat for a moment. What else could we try?'

or 'We have spent a lot of time wearing the black hat, what might be the yellow hat's view of this?'

- In a team meeting, you could have some fun with it by asking:

  'Who's most likely to wear each hat?'

Then mix it up: for the rest of the meeting, assign people a different *hat* from the one they'd usually wear and see what changes.

- When someone comes to you with a problem or feels stuck, try offering a different hat to encourage them to think differently. For example:

  'If you put the red hat on for a moment, what is your gut telling you?'

However you use it, the aim is the same: to notice the instinct to fix, slow things down and help bring in wider perspectives that might otherwise be missed.

Tool 2: Thinking about how to make the best use of your energy using the Circle of Control model

One of the biggest challenges when we feel stuck or overwhelmed is the urge to solve everything all at once. We try to keep hold of all the options and control every variable. Our worry spills into everything (including the things we *can't* influence) because despite what we might tell ourselves, not everything is within our control.

We have a finite amount of energy and attention. And when we focus it on the things we *can't* influence, it doesn't just drain us and leave us feeling frustrated or even more overwhelmed; it also robs us of the time and energy we could use on the things we *can* do something about.

This is where the Circle of Control model helps.

Popularised by Stephen Covey, the model helps us pause, sort through what's going on and make more conscious choices about where to focus our energy. It's not about ignoring what's outside your control; it's about being more intentional with your effort, attention and influence (all of which use your energy).

The three parts to the model are:

1. **The Circle of Control:** the things you have full control over (such as your actions, what you prioritise, the decisions you make, how you respond to situations).

2. **The Circle of Influence:** the things you don't have full control over but may be able to affect (such as how you communicate, how you build relationships, how you support others).
3. **The Circle of Concern:** the things that feel important, but you can't do anything about (such as other people's decisions, external events affecting your work or wider organisational changes such as a restructure).

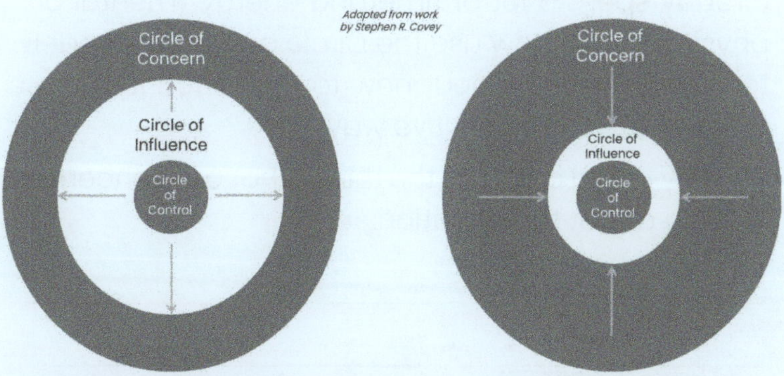

A) Our energy can be used on things we can influence and therefore more can be used positively

B) Our energy is placed more on the things we can't influence and therefore isn't used as impactfully

Imagine your total energy as the large outer circle on this diagram. Where you place that energy has a huge impact.

In A, when you focus on your Circle of Influence (or Control), you're putting energy into the things you can do something about. Covey calls this a *proactive focus*, placing positive energy where it can make a difference. As a result, your Circle of Influence expands.

In B, when you focus on what you *can't* control, you're still using up energy, but you're also shrinking your Circle of Influence. Covey calls this a *reactive focus* because you're using your energy on things you can't change.

Neither is about ignoring what's happening. But A helps you make progress and B keeps you stuck.

Putting it into practice

Think about a situation that you're dealing with that feels overwhelming or frustrating, maybe something you feel stuck on, even though you've already spent a lot of time and energy (mental or physical) on it. Now use the Circle of Control model to help you think about how to approach it in the most positive or *proactive* way.

Start by listing out all of the things that are concerning you about this situation:

____

____

____

Then ask yourself (honestly): 'What's actually within my control here?'

(The things I can act on or change myself, eg the choices or decisions I am making, my behaviour or my mindset.)

____

____

____

What might I be able to influence?

(The things I don't have full control over but could affect, eg a conversation I could have, a relationship I could repair.)

____

____

____

What's outside of my control?

(Things I might care about or might be important, but I can't do anything about, eg a decision someone else has made, an action someone else has taken.)

____

____

____

Now reflect on what you have written.

Where has most of your energy been put so far?

____

____

____

What would need to happen for you to move more into your Circle of Control or Influence?

____

____

____

What's the first step you want to take as a result?

____

____

____

Tool 3: Getting clear and creative using the Creative Problem Solving (CPS) technique

It's not always a lack of answers or options that keeps us stuck; it's that we're solving the wrong problem in the first place.

We might be focusing on symptoms and missing the underlying cause. Or we might be reacting to the most obvious issue rather than thinking about what really needs to change.

For example, you might think that the problem is that your team keep missing deadlines, so you jump straight to implementing new project management software. But the real issue might be that priorities keep shifting or that they're being pulled into work outside their role due to under-resourced teams elsewhere. If you went with the initial solution, it probably wouldn't have much impact.

The Creative Problem Solving framework (Isaksen, Dorval & Treffinger 2011) offers a structured way to get clear on the problem (so your solution actually makes a difference), while also helping you think creatively about possible options and narrow them down so you can take action. We like to think of it as *giving shape to creative thinking*.

You don't want to shut ideas down too early or limit possibilities, but you also don't want to think without limits forever. This approach helps you to do both and can be particularly helpful when the challenge is complex, unclear or you keep going around in circles.

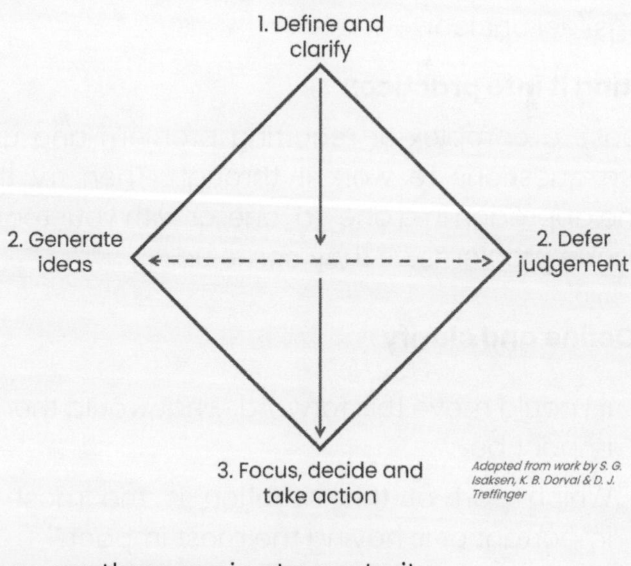

Adapted from work by S. G. Isaksen, K. B. Dorval & D. J. Treffinger

There are three main stages to it:

1. Define and clarify

Get clear on the *real* problem you're trying to solve (not just the one you started with). Write it as a *what* or *how* question and this becomes your *problem statement.*

2. Generate ideas and defer judgement

Let ideas flow without ruling anything out yet, aiming at this stage for quantity and diversity and not prioritising quality just yet.

3. Focus, decide and take action

Then come back out of the clouds. Start testing, prioritising and building out the best ideas into something you can act on.

You can use it for yourself, or support others when things feel unclear.

Putting it into practice:

Choose a complex or recurring problem and use these questions to work it through. Then try the same approach in a one-to-one, or with your team, to tackle problems as they come up.

1. Define and clarify

- If I could move this forward, what would the impact be?
- Which part of this situation is the most important or is having the most impact?
- What are the symptoms of the issue, and what might be the real cause?

- What's the actual question I'm trying to answer?

Write your problem statement as a *what* or a *how* question.

____

____

____

2. Generate and defer judgement

- What are all the possible options?
- And what are some more?
- What has worked elsewhere?
- If I were being brave, bold or creative, what might I try?

Capture at least ten options, and when you think you're done, capture three more.

If you're doing this as a team, try using sticky notes, setting a time limit or coming up with ideas using each letter of the alphabet... get creative about creative thinking!

____

____

____

3. Focus, decide and take action

- Which ideas feel exciting or promising?
- What could I try out to test a few of them?
- What might be the barriers I'd need to overcome?
- Which ones do I actually want to take forward?

If working as a team, consider grouping similar themes and ideas and then use sticky dots to vote and prioritise.

____

____

____

What's the first step you will take as a result?

____

____

____

Try this: a conversation for problem solving

Think of someone who regularly brings problems or decisions to you. Now think of a situation they're currently dealing with where, if you're honest, you're holding the hot potato (from page 71) either partially or fully for them.

Use the prompts below to plan for the next time it happens, so you can help them take more ownership.

What's your instinctive response when they come to you?

(What do you usually say or do?)

____

____

____

What assumptions are you making?

(About them, their ability, your role or what they need from you?)

____

____

____

If the next interaction was a success, what would be different?

(*What would change in what you both said or did?*)

___

___

___

How much do they know about your reflections above?

(*Have you shared your thinking or are you expecting them to guess?*)

___

___

___

What would a good balance of support and challenge look like in this conversation?

(*What might you say or do?*)

___

___

___

What might you need to name, or say out loud to shift the dynamic?

(*For example: I want to support you with this, but I also want you to know I believe you can figure it out.*)

____

____

____

What's one question you could ask the moment they come to you?

(*Something that stops you instinctively grabbing the hot potato?*)

____

____

____

How could you follow up in a way that keeps ownership with them?

(*Without taking it back again?*)

____

____

____

What's the first step you could take (or the first conversation you need to have) as a result of this reflection?

____

____

____

Final thought

You don't always have to take the role of *fixer* when a problem comes up. In fact, you can often have more impact by helping others work out the next step for themselves. That doesn't mean leaving people to flounder alone; it means taking a different role in the conversation: one where the other person holds responsibility for the problem and you help them to work through it.

And these conversations don't need to be long. Sometimes just one well-timed question is the difference between you grabbing the hot potato or them holding onto it and deciding what to do. Done well, these conversations don't just solve problems, they build capability, confidence and capacity. They send a clear message: you care what your team thinks, you believe in them and you trust them to handle the tricky stuff. Simply put, you're there to support but not rescue.

Now what?

Conversations aren't an add-on to leadership. They *are* the work of leadership. In a world of AI, hybrid work, multigenerational and global teams, and the challenges still to come, they matter more than ever.

Culture is built by the conversations we have and the ones we avoid. When you think about it that way, leadership stops being a performance and starts being a practice – one built through the conversations you have every day.

There are thousands of books on leadership: the theory, the research, the models. But we want to leave you with a final thought.

What if we stripped all the noise around leadership away? What would we be left with then?

Conversations. The human ones. The ones that make great work happen and the ones that keep us ready for whatever comes next.

So, which conversation will you choose to have now?

References

Chapter 1

Scott, S (2017) *Fierce Conversations: Achieving success in work and life, one conversation at a time*. Piatkus.

Chapter 2

Anagnostakis, A. The Vertical Development Institute. URL: verticaldevelopment.education

Burch, N (1970s) The Conscious Competence Ladder. URL: gordontraining.com/free-workplace-articles/learning-a-new-skill-is-easier-said-than-done

Dweck, C (2006) *Mindset: The new psychology of success*. Random House.

Banaji, M R & Greenwald, A G (2013) *Blindspot: Hidden biases of good people*. Delacorte Press.

Chapter 4

Downing, M (2014) *Effective Modern Coaching: The principles and art of successful business coaching*. LID Business Media.

Scott, K (2017) *Radical Candor: How to get what you want by saying what you mean*. Pan Macmillan.

Chapter 5

Brown, B (2015) *Daring Greatly: How the courage to be vulnerable transforms the way we live, love, parent, and lead.* Avery.

DISC:

- The theory was originally based on: Marston, W M (1928) *Emotions of Normal People*. Harcourt, Brace and Company.

- For a practical overview and applications: DISC Personality Testing: discprofile.com

Insights:

- Based on Jung's typology: Jung, C G (1921) *Psychological Types*. Rascher Verlag. (English translation 1971, Princeton University Press).
- For current use: Insights Discovery: Personality development and team effectiveness tool: insights.com

MBTI: based on Jung's typology (see above). For current use: Myers, I B, McCaulley, M H et al (1998) *MBTI® Manual: A guide to the development and use of the Myers-Briggs Type Indicator*. Consulting Psychologists Press.

Chapter 6

Boswell, W R, Bingham, J B and Colvin, A J S (2006) 'Aligning employees through "line of sight"'. Cornell University, ILR School. URL: digitalcommons.ilr.cornell.edu/articles/580

Chapter 7

Cantrell, S, et al (2024) 'When people thrive, business thrives: The case for human sustainability'. Deloitte Insights.

Luft, J & Ingham, H (1955) 'The Johari Window: A graphic model of interpersonal awareness'. Proceedings of the Western Training Laboratory in Group Development. University of California.

Humphrey, A (2005) 'SWOT Analysis for management consulting'. SRI Alumni Association Newsletter, December, pp 7–8.

Gestalt:

- Origins of Gestalt psychology: Wertheimer, M (1938) 'Laws of organization in perceptual forms'. In W D Ellis (ed, 1999) *A Source Book of*

Gestalt Psychology. London: Routledge & Kegan Paul

- For a leadership/organisational lens: Nevis, E C (1987) *Organizational Consulting: A Gestalt approach*. Gestalt Institute of Cleveland Press.

Chapter 8

Pugh, M (2017) 'Chairwork in cognitive behavioural therapy'. URL: chairwork.co.uk

Landsberg, M (1996) *The Tao of Coaching: Boost your effectiveness at work by inspiring and developing those around you*. HarperCollins.

Center for Creative Leadership (nd). The SBI Feedback Model. URL: ccl.org

Woodruffe, C (2006) 'Development and assessment centres: Identifying and developing competence'. CIPD.

Heen, S and Stone, D (2014) 'Find the coaching in criticism'. *Harvard Business Review*, January.

Scott, S (2017) – see Chapter 1.

Chapter 9

Whitmore, J (1992) *Coaching for Performance: A practical guide to growing your own skills*. Nicholas Brealey.

Hawkins, P (2011) *Creating a Coaching Culture*. McGraw-Hill/Open University Press.

Gilbert, A & Whittleworth, K (2002) The OSCAR Coaching Model. Coaching & Mentoring Network. URL: coaching-network.org.uk

de Bono, E (1985) *Six Thinking Hats*. Little, Brown and Company.

Covey, S R (1989) *The 7 Habits of Highly Effective People: Powerful lessons in personal change*. Free Press.

Isaksen, S G, Dorval, K B & Treffinger, D J (2011) *Creative Approaches to Problem Solving: A framework for innovation and change* (3rd ed). SAGE Publications.

About the authors

Naomi Regan and Lynsey Kitching are leadership development consultants, facilitators and coaches, and co-founders of CAPE People Development, specialising in helping leaders build workplace cultures shaped by everyday conversations.

Naomi began her career leading multi-million-pound infrastructure programmes and shaping strategy in complex organisations. This experience taught her that leadership isn't about expertise, but about the impact you have on others – one conversation at a time – grounding her practical, human approach to leadership development. Known for her vibrant, high-energy style, she has designed and delivered hundreds of leadership programmes and completed more than 1,500 coaching hours, helping leaders shift from knowing what good leadership looks like to actually doing it. She also serves as a charity trustee, strengthening culture, people strategy and leadership capability. Outside work, she's happiest with her family, exploring creative ideas or dipping into cold water.

Lynsey started her career in corporate property before moving into communications, organisational change and strategy. This taught her how vital it is to help people navigate complexity, uncertainty and competing pressures. She now specialises in helping leaders succeed through practical, meaningful conversations that create clarity, connection and confidence, bringing a grounded, human approach to every room she's in. Known for her calm clarity, curiosity and thoughtful challenge, she helps clients uncover what's holding them back and take purposeful action. She also holds a post-graduate qualification in organisational leadership from Oxford Saïd Business School. Outside work, she's happiest with her daughters and taking on sporting challenges.

Together, Naomi and Lynsey have supported organisations across sectors and around the globe, coached thousands of hours and designed countless leadership programmes – all centred on one belief: leadership is lived in the conversations you have, and the ones you avoid. And when leaders master those everyday conversations, they unlock their greatest competitive advantage.